Phil Myers
7/90

LESLIE PARROTT

Softly and Tenderly

THE ALTAR—
A Place
to Encounter God

BEACON HILL PRESS OF KANSAS CITY

KANSAS CITY, MISSOURI

Permission to quote from the following copyrighted versions is acknowledged with
appreciation:

The Holy Bible, New International Version (NIV), copyright © 1973, 1978, 1984 by
the International Bible Society.

The *New King James Version* (NKJV), copyright © 1979, 1980, 1982, Thomas Nelson,
Inc., Publishers.

The *Revised Standard Version of the Bible* (RSV), copyrighted 1946, 1952, © 1971,
1973.

The Living Bible (TLB), © 1971 by Tyndale House Publishers, Wheaton, Ill.

10   9   8   7   6   5   4   3   2   1

This book is dedicated
to the good people in the little stone church
at
Monterey, Tenn.,
where my grandparents, Tom and Samantha Parrott,
prayed and shouted around the altar,
and where my father, A. L. Parrott,
first entered his spiritual pilgrimage.

CONTENTS

Foreword

My good friend Les has produced a fine work that drew me back to some warm, fond memories that I have had at the altar. Those precious and memorable events have produced in me a positive attitude toward the altar that holds fast even today. I believe those landmarks, coupled with a study of the unquestionable biblical significance of the altar, developed my deep appreciation for this sacred, symbolic piece of furniture.

Dr. Parrott addresses the consideration whether altar calls can meet a need in churches today. Without hesitation this pastor unreservedly answers, "Yes!" I pastor in an action-packed, thrill-seeking, recreation-loving beach city in Southern California where more than 50 percent of my congregation is from unchurched backgrounds. Altar calls and public invitations are given frequently and with outstanding response. Why? I believe it is because of the atmosphere that has been created toward the altar.

This book is filled with wonderful history from the Old Testament, the New Testament, and the English and American reformers who brought back the use of the altar. There is no doubt that altar calls had significant impact in the lives of consecrated believers as well as unsaved seekers. But I challenge you: Do not limit your thinking toward the altar and altar calls for today!

There is a sense of solemnizing that takes place on bended knees before a crowd of witnesses (Matt. 10:32). For instance, our church regularly calls on visitors and prospects during the week. Quite commonly the living room sofa or dining room table becomes the altar where someone places his trust in Christ. But more frequently than not, this young believer has a desire to cement the new relationship at the altar the following Sunday. Why? I believe it is a sense of permanence and sacredness—much like the exchange of wedding vows.

I am in agreement with Dr. Parrott concerning the tie between the altar rail and the pulpit. The author's interviews and surveys with fast- and slow-growing churches reflect that correlation. I firmly believe everything rises and falls on the leadership of the church, and the pastor has the ability to educate the congregation toward positive feelings about the altar. Without the experience and receptivity toward an open altar, a body of believers will miss many treasured encounters with God.

For me, going to the altar is much like going to the family dinner table as a young boy. There was a sense of openness, transparency, love, and tenderness. My parents read my face and drew out my need to release fears, pain, frustrations, and even disobedience. I sensed unconditional love at that table and was welcomed to share my deepest longings and greatest needs. Isn't that why we need to go to the altar?

Pastor or layperson, my prayer and hope for you is that your heart will be open to the ministry of this book and that your life will be further transformed through the practice of seeking the face of God at the altar.

—John C. Maxwell, Senior Pastor
Skyline Wesleyan Church

Preface

Tracing the idea of the altar and assessing its current significance has provided me with more than a year of study and inspiration. The sacred altar in our churches is not only the place of encounter with God but also the place where we face ourselves in the mirror of God's love. As a fine black preacher in St. Louis put it in one of our interviews, "In our church the altar is a sign of our trust in God and not a sign of our failure."

This work is addressed to all the people who love the church altar as a means of grace. It is not written for those who have forsaken the public altar and are self-conscious about the idea of a public invitation. Their concern with the altar is likely the symptom of a theological problem. This book is written for those who welcome the altar as a convenient place for encounter with God.

The idea of an international church in a highly nationalistic world gives pause for thought in declaring the public altar an American idea. But it is. The Anglican Communion rail was used in England in the 18th century, although there is no indication Wesley used it as an altar for penitents. It may be that the Salvation Army altar in the late 1800s came via America with only an adoptive birthright in England. However, my reading of academic dissertations and published literature on the public invitation leads me to agree with Dr. Robert Coleman, the distinguished Methodist scholar on evangelism, who declares the altar to be a unique American phenomenon.

In any case, the origins of the altar should not be a stumbling block for international use any more than Wesleyanism should be confined to England because it originated there, or Luther's pulpit restricted to Germany because Luther was a German. Like Abraham Lincoln, who "belongs to the ages," the love of the altar as a means of grace belongs to those pietistic Christians, wherever they are in the world, who see the altar as a place of spiritual encounter.

Most of us will find Divisions Four and Five the most interesting because they deal with the altar we relate to now. I promised complete anonymity to the four pastors who gave me their stories in chapters 13—16, as well as the men I interviewed for chapters 11 and 12. I will always be grateful to the members of the six focus groups who identified the issues and concerns in chapter 10. Without changing the substance, I have moved to conceal the identities of all the people in chapters 10 through 16, believing the promise of anonymity would make persons more bold in telling me what they really think about the altar.

The first nine chapters are a necessary prelude to Divisions Four and Five. Instead of focusing on the physical structure of the altar in wood or stone, I have tried to trace the idea of the altar through the Bible and church history. Noah built the first altar just after the Flood, and the latest altars are still under construction in the churches of today and tomorrow. But regardless of how we feel about the ways, means, and methods of the altar then and now, we must always remind ourselves that Christ is both our Altar and our High Priest.

There is a reason why I omitted Dwight L. Moody, Billy Sunday, and Billy Graham from this study even though they are three of the greatest evangelists in American history. This is not a book about evangelism but a book about the altar and evangelism that focuses on the altar. Moody used the warm-hearted appeal of the Methodist invitation but resisted the altar in favor of a prayer room. Billy Sunday focused on the handshake as a symbol of intention. He had a little elevator built into the platform so that he could be lowered down to aisle level where he welcomed thousands of people into the Kingdom with a handshake. I have never heard of Billy Graham using the public altar in any of his crusades, although he joined a church that uses the altar for evangelism. If we were studying the public invitation, these men would have been included. However, since we are focused on the altar, I omitted them.

No one can do a study of this kind without involving many people. In differing ways, a great number of people deserve more gratitude than I can express in this introduction:

If it had not been for the continuing encouragement of Dr. Bill Sullivan, this project would never have been undertaken, let alone finished.

I want to thank Mrs. Ruth Kinnersley in the library of Olivet Nazarene University, who stretched the limits of the computerized interlibrary loan system to secure my reading list, and especially the Ph.D. dissertations that became a gold mine in source material.

Every writer needs someone with a Ph.D. in English to mend his faults in the use of words. I have an on-campus editor of exceptional skills in a good friend and faculty member, Dr. Larry Finger.

And, of course, there is never a finished manuscript without the endless work on a word processor by a dedicated professional. Thanks to Mrs. Jan Royal. This was her second book-length manuscript, and she did excellent work again.

This book does not have all the answers. It was not written with final answers in mind. The ultimate value and meaning of the kneeling altar as a means of grace rests in the heart of the beholder. The purpose of this book is to focus our attention on the possibilities of a new encounter. May God make it so.

DIVISION ONE

In the Beginning

Softly and tenderly Jesus is calling,
  Calling for you and for me.
See, on the portals He's waiting and watching,
  Watching for you and for me.
    —from the hymn "Softly and Tenderly"

1

The Idea of
a Public Altar

IN THE CHURCH where I grew up, nothing was more important than the altar. Most of the sermons were beyond me, except for an occasional story or the histrionics of a visiting evangelist whose novelty was compelling to a child. We had no organ. The choir was limp except for high notes. We had a Communion table but seldom had Communion. And when we did, it was served in the seats.

But when it came to the altar, that was entirely another matter. Even the length of our altar was dramatic: straight as an arrow, stretching across the full width of the church, not even affording access to the Communion table or the pulpit with an appropriate break in the center on the sanctuary level. What went on at that altar was powerful and impressive. People broke through from great sorrow to great joy; they got rid of guilt, received forgiveness, and were filled with the Holy Spirit. And all of these individualized experiences happened simultaneously. The testimonies that followed were as dramatic and powerful as the praying itself.

Although I was spellbound by what happened at our altar, I was also embarrassed. For the sake of ventilation, we had a side door, right at the end of our altar on the street side, where outsiders sometimes gathered and watched the spiritual drama play itself out. When kids at school asked me about the noisy people and their loud prayers, I had a hard time explaining.

On Sunday nights and during revival, I always secured a front seat for myself. That first row advantage was as important to me during my childhood as a seat on the first base line is for a Chicago Cubs fan. I knew where the action was, and I intended to be there. I learned early on that the success of the sermon depended on what happened during the altar call. As I got older and started reading church news in the official denominational paper, I was not surprised that the highlight in every revival report was the number of seekers at the altar, "counting them as they came."

It never entered my mind that the idea of an altar and the public invitation were uniquely American. I took it for granted that Jesus and the apostles had an altar, though not as long and straight as ours. To me, the altar at the front of the church was a given: It existed now, it always had existed, and it always would exist as a chief place to encounter God.

I loved the altar. I was disappointed when they demolished the church to make way for a bigger sanctuary and destroyed the altar where I knelt as a penitent child to accept Christ as Lord of my life.

The story of my spiritual pilgrimage could be charted by the succession of spiritual encounters I had at the altar. I guess my first encounter came when my mother and father took me to the altar to be dedicated as a baby. I was saved and later sanctified at the altar and returned during revival times for new touches, new assurances, and new spiritual advances. During the teen years I fought and won battles on the standards of my adolescent behavior during new encounters at the altar. I bought the idea that the altar in our church was not the place to go in final desperation but the reference point of first opportunity during times of spiritual concern.

Lora Lee and I were pronounced husband and wife at the altar of the church with a sanctuary full of friends as witnesses to our exchange of vows. I was ordained at the altar of prayer by a general superintendent whose earnest prayer still rings in my memories. The press of his hands on my head still lingers in my mind as both a restraining force and a motivational touch.

We buried my father and, some years later, my mother from the altar of the church where they were charter members. Their commitment to the church was directly related to the importance of the altar and its use.

All three of our sons were born anew of the Spirit at familiar altars. They were married at the altars of churches where their brides had grown up with their own love of the altar and their own histories of its place in their spiritual encounters. And now two grandsons have been dedicated at church altars where their father is pastor.

And so the cycle of personal and family encounters with the church altar keeps on rolling like a stream with an artesian source, watering the lives of those who kneel to drink from its renewing flow. To eliminate the altar from my Christian pilgrimage would be like taking the Wesley hymns out of the hymnbook or the Gospels out of the Bible.

But something happened to make me wonder about this church altar I had taken for granted as part and parcel of every Christian's heritage. I knew that the Catholic church in our community had a different kind of altar from ours, but after all, they were different from our church in lots of other ways too. I knew that a school chum's father, who was pastor of the Baptist church, had a special room for praying instead of an altar. But I saw this as an evident lack of their spiritual courage. If Christ died in the open, could we do any less than walk down an aisle and kneel at a public altar for His forgiveness and renewal?

Then I made a trip to England.

I may not have known much about church history and even less about serious theology, but I did know that John Wesley was our spiritual godfather, and whatever he said or did had the ring of authority. In this frame of mind, I went to Bristol where Wesley preached and where the great 18th-century revival began. This was the revival that changed

England's history and gave America its largest Protestant denomination. I arrived in Bristol filled with anticipation and enjoying a high level of expectation.

From my background of the American altar, I expected to see the same, or similar, altar in Wesley's gathering place where this historic revival began. To my utter dismay there was none, not even a Communion rail. I thought the altar might have been out for repairs or refinishing. But alas, it was out because it had never been in.

I sought out the sexton in charge of the New Room and asked him about John Wesley's altar. That's right: There was none. "Mr. Wesley didn't use an altar like you Americans," he said.

"Then what did he do?" I asked naively, setting myself up for a shocking rejoinder.

"I guess he just depended on the Holy Spirit," the sexton said, turning his back on me as he walked away.

In some small way, that experience in the New Room in Bristol may have been the genesis of the motivation for the study that has produced this volume. If the old-fashioned altar as we know it in America is our own invention, how did we get the idea? Even more important, what need did we have that produced the altar, need being the mother of invention? And what about all the altars mentioned in the Bible? Are our altars and the altars in the Bible totally disconnected, or do they mirror each other? And what about the public invitation? Is that an American idea too? Did Jesus and the apostles not have a proclamation that brought people to a decision on spiritual matters? And where did the Catholics, the Episcopalians, and the Lutherans get their kinds of altars? Are they all wrong, and we all right? And how important is the altar now? Will it be used and loved as I have known it? Or is the idea of the altar fading? With these and other questions, I began to read, talk, and listen.

I'll drop to the bottom line and then take the rest of this book to fill you in on the process. The kneeling altar, in combination with the pulpit and the Communion table, is still the most important piece of furniture in our churches.

The idea of an altar in front of the pulpit is uniquely American, but after 200 years of spiritual use it has almost become indigenous in parishes far removed from the golden shores of North America. As the church is further internationalized, there is more need for understanding the meaning and the purposes of the altar. It is time for a new encounter.

An Australian Transplant

At the end of World War II young people in the Church of the Nazarene launched a fund-raising project for building churches in Australia. Their motivation may have come partially from gratitude for the Australian soldiers who were our loyal comrades during battles in the South Pacific. And it may have been an expression of gratitude to the people of Australia who became friends to great numbers of American servicemen who passed through their cities. Or the move among young people to raise money for Australia may have been the unknowing beginning of a great internationalization move in the Church of the Nazarene.

In 1946, when E. E. Zachary and his family arrived in Sydney, New South Wales, to put the project on line, Hardy Powers had been a general superintendent for only two years. G. B. Williamson was elected in a mail vote that same year, and Samuel Young joined his colleagues in the general superintendency in 1948. These men formed a formidable alliance of vision, persistence, and persuasiveness that was needed to change the thinking of the people from national to international. It was more than missions; it was a new way of looking at the world. The 10 percent General Budget was no small factor in this surge for global concern. But somewhere near the beginning of this entire process was the Australia project.

The Zacharys were greeted at dockside by four men who were the Australian connection down under. A. A. E. Berg was an army man who had been deeply influenced toward holiness and the Spirit-filled life by an enlisted comrade during the war years. He brought with him three other men whom he was discipling in the ministry. A. A. Clarke and A. C. Chesson were from Sydney, and W. D. Pinch was from the outback where he had done Christian work with the aborigines. These four men, along with E. E. Zachary, would be central to this work on the continent down under. But the catalyst for this spiritual movement was to be an altar service.

Services began in a place called Baker's Hall on Beamish Street in Campsie, a suburb of Sydney. Although these four men had read about altars and altar services, none of them had ever seen or been in one. These young Australian leaders were anxious, uninitiated in matters relating to the altar, but prayerfully expectant. But finally the time came. After a week of services characterized mostly by questions and answers with much open discussion and reading of literature on the sanctified life, the time came. Hear it in Dr. Zachary's own words:

> As I recall, it was on a Thursday night of the second week of our meetings when I felt the Lord directing me to extend the first invitation for seekers at the altar. I asked the men to set out six chairs, facing the audience, to be used for an altar. If God could give us six seekers in this first altar service—seekers who would really pray through—I thought it would be a great spiritual advance.
>
> As the people were gathering for the service, I heard someone ask one of the pastors, "Are we having special singers tonight?"
>
> "No. Our American brother has asked us to set these chairs for an altar where people can pray through."
>
> "Pray through chairs? Whatever for?"
>
> And the pastor replied, "Our American brother will explain."
>
> As a prologue to the evening message, I spoke briefly about altars in the Bible. I explained their symbolism. I explained how they were built by human effort as places for meeting God and especially for offering sacrifices. Then I explained how God sent His Son, Jesus Christ, as the ultimate Sacrifice, sufficient for all our sins.

I told them we had set out the chairs as an altar where we could kneel in prayer and accept His sacrifice for our sins. I said, I would be willing to pray with those who came forward after the sermon to be forgiven of their sins or to consecrate themselves for the infilling of the Holy Spirit.

I then invited the congregation to read selected scriptures with me from John's great passages on the Holy Spirit, John 14—17. Our attitude was prayerful as we read the instructions of Jesus to His disciples and the promises He made them concerning the Holy Spirit, who would be their Comforter, Teacher, Helper, and Sanctifier.

I paused in the reading to explain that these promises were not only to the disciples but also to all of us who accept Christ as Lord of our lives.

When I finally invited seekers to pray, the six chairs were filled, almost immediately. I asked the men to bring additional chairs. Every spare chair we had was finally pressed into service in our improvised altar as the people continued to come forward. To my surprise and joy, 26 persons knelt at that first altar.

Then it hit me: I was the only person present who had ever experienced an altar service. How could I be sure that their spiritual needs were met? How could I counsel and pray with every one personally? My silent prayer came with great sincerity: *Lord, help me. What can I do?*

I suddenly realized that the future of the altar service as a tool of the Holy Spirit in Australia did not depend solely on bringing the people forward, but equally on a supernatural visitation on each seeker. If nothing happened, the idea of the American altar as a transplant was dead.

I believe the Spirit led me. First, I asked the congregation to be seated and to pray. Then I placed the four preachers at intervals along the altar to pray with each seeker according to his need. I asked them to pray earnestly and loud enough to be heard by those kneeling at the altar. I felt that they needed to be heard at both ends of the altar. Each man did pray earnestly but much more briefly than I had in mind. In a matter of moments their prayers were ended, and there was no visible indication that anything spiritual was happening with the seekers.

In quiet desperation I cried out again, *Lord, help us. Lord, what can I do?*

The answer to my prayer came in a beautiful inner surge of reassurance and direction: This is My service. All you need to do is go to the end of the altar and, beginning with the first seeker, pray for each one, as individuals, to receive the Holy Spirit; and I will do the rest.

How can I describe the coming of the Holy Spirit? Holy fire? Rushing wind? Waves of glory? It was all of these, but mostly it was a sense of a spiritual Presence. As I moved along the row of praying people, I had come to about the third or fourth person when all of the above broke in on us. Beginning at my right where I had already prayed, there came audible sounds of sobs and praises. The sounds and feelings rose up from the thin line of people, along the full length of the altar across the entire front of our meetinghouse. It was too marvelous for words. Then the congregation bridged the gap between the front row and the improvised altar as they joined in the tears of joy and sounds of praise. No one was spiritually unmoved.

Under special assignment, a decade later, I returned to Australia as the presiding chairman of the 10th Annual District Assembly. While there, I made it my responsibility to find out how many of those who were sanctified in that first altar service could still be accounted for. Twenty-four were accounted for as steadfast with the Lord and still in the church. The remaining 2 of the original 26 had gone on to heaven.

If the lasting quality of the spiritual transformation and an enduring Christian commitment are the tests of religious experience, the first altar service in Sydney must be a heartwarming story in God's Book of Memories.

There is an addendum to the story of the first Nazarene altar service in Australia. An amazing follow-up experience came during the First Annual District Assembly. The place was Campsie again. The time was Sunday morning, April 4, 1948. The occasion was the morning worship service. The following account is taken directly from the district journal as prepared by the district secretary:

> The morning service opened at 11:00. The singing was in charge of Rev. S. G. Simmons. Our district superintendent, Rev. E. E. Zachary, led the assembly in a gracious Communion service. The people gathered around the altar for prayer and meditation on the Cross as Brother Zachary and the pastors assisted in serving the Communion elements.
>
> During this time of worship there was great solemnity upon the meeting. Hearts were blessed as they knelt before the Lord in this memorial of His death. Following this, Brother Zachary baptized a young lady, then dedicated the lovely children of Pastors Simmons and Pinch.
>
> During the singing of a special number in song, the Holy Ghost fell upon the congregation in a way heretofore unknown in Australia. His power and presence was great and wonderful. There was weeping, laughing, and shouts of praise.
>
> During this wonderful manifestation, seekers came to the altar. The mighty blessing continued through the altar service when all seekers came through. A testimony followed in the same spirit. Hearts were melted and blessed. Our people can now say they have seen the manifestation of Pentecostal power.
>
> This came, we feel, as a seal upon the work of the Church of the Nazarene in spreading scriptural holiness throughout Australia. Many had read about such scenes, but none had heretofore seen such an outpouring of Holy Ghost power.

Today there are more than 50 Nazarene churches in Australia and New Zealand with an equal cohort of ordained ministers and God-sent missionaries representing them in the international thrust of the church. Near Brisbane there is a thriving Bible college training young men and women for ministry. But it all began with the vision of young people in the United States and the catalyst of a significant altar service, plus the confirming of the Holy Spirit poured out in a

Sunday morning Communion worship service during the first district assembly.

A Baptist Encounter

Since Lora Lee and I have three sons in the ministry, we never lack for updates on what's happening in their segment of the church. They phone home irregularly, but on a two- or three-times-a-month basis, usually to check up on family news, exchange pleasantries, and report on what is happening in each of their private worlds.

Not long ago, while I was writing this manuscript, the middle son, Roger, phoned from Dallas, where he had gone on church business. He was more excited than I had heard him for a long time. He talked more rapidly than usual, and there was an unmistakable melody in his voice that told me he had special news.

Roger's news was about an altar in a place known for its spiritual concern and about a man who had the stature of Goliath but the heart of David. He said, "Instead of telling you my story, I want to write it out, and you'll get it in a few days." And sure enough, I did. I could rewrite Roger's story and even personalize it with a phone call to Dallas. But I think it is best to let him tell the story in his own words:

> In my work with the Lausanne Committee for World Evangelization, I had the privilege of calling on Dr. W. A. Criswell, the patriarchal pastor of the First Baptist Church of Dallas. I met him in his office late on a Friday afternoon, and even at 83 years of age, his energy, vitality, and godly spirit reflected the sanctified personality that has made him a giant among spiritual leaders. His church has enjoyed phenomenal growth that has earned the congregation and the pastor an international reputation.
>
> During our conversation, I mentioned to Dr. Criswell that I was a Nazarene minister, and immediately he began to share with me a most fascinating story about a dramatic change in his ministry because of what he ex-

perienced on a Nazarene campground and how the change affected Dallas First Baptist and then great numbers of other Baptist churches around the world.

Dr. Criswell told me that more than 30 years ago he was invited to the West Coast to preach to a group of Baptist ministers. He was told in advance that the pastors were discouraged and frustrated because of slow growth in their churches and were coming together for a Monday-through-Friday revival just for themselves—no laymen. Arrangements had been made to hold the services on a Nazarene campground south of San Francisco at a place called Beulah Park at Santa Cruz.

Dr. Criswell said that he saw the long altar across the front of the tabernacle, the first thing when he walked in. At that time, he said, no Baptist church had an altar, but the leaders of the revival decided to leave the altar in place. It wouldn't hurt anything.

As the week wore on, little progress was being made toward breaking the discouragement of the ministers, although they continued to pray together and wait on the Lord for help. However, on Thursday night of that revival something unique did happen. Just as Dr. Criswell began his sermon for the evening, a pastor arose and walked from his seat in the congregation to the altar and knelt down to pray. Since this was something new for a Baptist meeting, Dr. Criswell said he wasn't sure what to do. So he just kept on preaching.

As the sermon continued, so did the seekers. Another minister came forward to pray, and then another, and another. Soon the altar was lined with ministers seeking God in earnest prayer. The spiritual results of that service were powerful enough to encourage the discouraged Baptist preachers, and dramatic enough to change Dr. Criswell's thinking about the altar as a means of grace in the church. There was something different about men kneeling at the public altar that couldn't be achieved in a more private prayer room. While watching those men pray, Dr. Criswell determined in his mind to recommend to his Board of Deacons that they install an altar in his church, Dallas First Baptist.

Although Dr. Criswell's determination to have an altar did not waver, his desire was not sufficiently supported by his nerve. Since no Baptist church had an altar, and since his people had not been accustomed to an altar, he was afraid of the reaction he would get from his board. So, board meeting after board meeting, he delayed recommending the installation of an altar.

However, a letter came to Dr. Criswell that spurred him into action. It came from the pastor who was the first man to walk down the aisle to the altar on that Thursday evening during the revival for discouraged pastors at Santa Cruz. The pastor apologized to Dr. Criswell for disrupting the service, but explained that a critical time had come to him, since he and his wife had already decided to leave the ministry for secular work. He was planning to resign on the next Sunday morning following the revival. But in his letter, written six months after Dr. Criswell's revival, the pastor said that God changed those plans at the altar of prayer in Beulah Park, and since that altar service his ministry had taken on new life and joy.

With the letter of encouragement in hand, Dr. Criswell decided the time had come to recommend the installation of the altar. He would do it at the next regular board meeting. And he did. The reaction of the board was just what he expected—stony silence. They had heard him tell the story of the altar at Beulah Park, but none of them had been there. Finally one of the deacons broke the chilling silence. Clearing his throat and straightening up in his chair, the man said, "If our pastor believes we should have a mourner's bench in this church, I'm sure it is of God."

With his story ended, Dr. Criswell moved forward in his chair and, building the intensity of his voice, said to me, "My Nazarene friend, tell your church to never allow the altar to become only a piece of furniture in your church, but keep using it and making it a place where people find God."

Dr. Criswell told me there were now thousands of Baptist churches that have followed the lead of Dallas First Baptist by installing altars in their sanctuaries. And through the example of the Nazarenes, he said, their churches have grown, and their worship has been enriched by their altars.

After we had prayed together in his office at the conclusion of our business, Dr. Criswell asked me to go with him across the street to the sanctuary so that he could show me the altar. And of course I did. After 30 years, the wood was worn and the fabric somewhat stained. But for a moment, I knelt at the altar of that great Baptist church and thanked God for all the Nazarene altars that have meant so much to my spiritual walk as Dr. Criswell prayed for me and for my church.

The Need for a New Encounter

Maybe it is time for great numbers of churches and the host of individuals who make up the congregations to have a new encounter with the altar. Some old-line churches have eliminated the altar because they have eliminated concern for repentance, restitution, new birth, spiritual growth, the sanctified life, and the special times that call for renewed Christian commitment. Other evangelical churches have no need for the altar because they have inquiry rooms for those kinds of prayers. Still other churches haven't eliminated the altar; they have just let it be relegated to a role of little meaning and lost purpose. But with a great host of us, the altar is a precious and important piece of sacred furniture that provides the place in worship for new encounters of a spiritual nature.

*   *   *

Some time ago I was walking through the bedroom toward the dressing room when a sideways glance caught the name of a book lying on Lora Lee's side of the big, king-size, overhead brass bed where we sleep. The title so startled me that I stopped, picked up the book, and began to examine it. The title was *Life with a Difficult Man*. To my relief, the book was about the wife of Jonathan Edwards and her struggles in the parsonage with an intense Calvinist preacher-husband.

I have great respect for Jonathan Edwards and his theological shift that opened the window on personal responsibility in salvation for New England Calvinists. He was an earnest man who did much good. But all of us who love the altar know there is another branch in the evangelical stream in America that does not lead to Jonathan Edwards but to John Wesley and beyond. We gather on the Arminian side of the river to examine the meaning, purpose, and development of the altar as a means of grace in our churches.

We trace the heritage of our altar back through the great holiness camp meetings after the Civil War, back through the public invitations of Dwight L. Moody (although he used an inquiry room), back through the revivals and new measures of Charles G. Finney in the state of New York, and finally back to the Methodist mourner's bench used in the camp meetings that followed the spiritual explosion at Cane Ridge, Ky., in 1801. It was the early Methodists under the leadership of Bishop Asbury and his circuit-riding preachers who brought the altar into common acceptance for many thousands of people.

In some places today, we need a new encounter with the altar to bring it into sharper focus as a means of grace. When we ignore the altar, we substitute signals of decision such as congregations of bowed heads with eyes lifted to respond to the preacher, or hands raised where people sit, or simply the admonition for people with needs to pray and seek spiritual counseling.

The altar is mentioned 433 times in the Bible, beginning with Noah. Every Old Testament leader beginning with Abraham, through the patriarchs, Moses, kings, and prophets, was an altar builder who experienced special encounters with God.

In the New Testament Christ our Lord became the final sacrificial Lamb whose blood redeems every person who comes to Him in faith. We have an altar who is Christ the Lord. In the early days of the plain, simple gospel, men came to Christ for healing, for forgiveness, and for the new birth. According to our Lord, the altar sanctified the gift (Matt. 23:19).

But in the centuries following the dominance of the Roman church, there occurred a great shift in matters relating to salvation. The pope became Christ's vicar. The church held the power of salvation through offering or withholding the benefits of the Mass. The pulpit was replaced by the altar that took the form of a beautiful high table in the sanctuary where the bread and wine were changed into the actual body and blood of our Lord. Under the Roman church, salvation through the call to a personal faith in Christ was abandoned in favor of political strategies. In a very real sense, the church at Rome inherited the monolithic structure of the Roman Empire and held that authority for more than 1,000 years.

By 1517 the Reformers were on the move. They led the church in magnificent theological changes. Luther brought us back to justification by faith. Calvin brought back to light the biblical idea of salvation by grace alone without works. And James Arminius led us into salvation by faith through grace available to all who believe.

But it was up to the Wesley brothers in England, Jonathan Edwards in America, and their colleague George Whitefield, who preached in both England and America, to be the forerunners of the public invitation and the altar.

In America some say the altar was used for the first time in 1807 or 1808 in a crowded New York chapel. Others say the first public invitation was made in Virginia. But regardless of who gave the very first invitation or prayed with the first seeker at a public altar, it was the Methodists who made it a uniquely American idea. They had an altar in every church. Thousands were saved and great hosts were sanctified at these Methodist altars, especially during the half century before the Civil War. Then, in the decades following the war, something happened. First the doctrine of holiness as understood by Asbury was subdued, then ignored, opposed, and ultimately rejected. And along with this trend went the altar.

This book is not for those who have rejected the altar but for those who love it, who pray for its preservation, and who believe in all the sacred altar stands for.

In 1910 Billy Sunday made a long trip for that time, all the way to the Pacific Northwest, where he conducted a series of citywide campaigns. When he arrived in Everett, Wash., some miles north of Seattle, he heard people talking about a sawdust trail used by the loggers to find their way home from isolated logging sites in the mountains.

There are several versions of the story, but according to one report, Billy Sunday, on a day off, actually went with the lumbermen into the forests of the Cascade Mountains to see the sawdust trail for himself. After the men were past familiar guideposts near their base camp, a logger used his knife to cut a hole in the large sack of red sawdust on the back of one of the pack animals. Throughout the trip into the dense fir forest, the trickle of sawdust on the ground was kept flowing by punching additional holes in additional bags as needed.

The men seemed in no hurry to get started home before dark. They built a fire, cooked a meal, and rested until they were ready to return. As they left the camping area, the men lighted their lanterns and with great confidence followed the sawdust trail back home.

The spiritual application of the sawdust trail struck Billy Sunday like a bolt. He ordered sawdust to be strewn down the aisles of his revival tabernacle, and then began inviting sinners to come home by hitting the sawdust trail.

In some ways, that is what this book is about. It is not for people who don't want to come home. It's not for people who are angry with the folks back home. However, if you love the church and believe in the altar, this book is an invitation for a new encounter with the most important piece of furniture in our churches. Let's examine the spiritual trail blazed through church history to give us the altar and the public invitation. Then let's examine both new and continuing encounters with the altar as a means of grace in worship and evangelism. As a starting place, let's turn next to the meaning of altars in the Bible.

2

Altars
in the Bible

THE SAGA of the altar in religious history began wherever man lived when he first felt the need to encounter God in a special way. It was probably somewhere in the Tigris-Euphrates River Valley, or in the surrounding hills, that some seeker built an altar, hoping to encounter God. No one knows where. But one fact is certain: This sacred sojourn of the altar began long before the electronic church, when listeners are asked by spellbinding speakers to put their hands on the television set as a point of contact.

The altar story predates any plans for mass evangelism in great stadiums where hundreds of seekers are expected nightly to stream forward for literature and a sinner's prayer made by the evangelist.

Long before there were local church revivals, tent meetings, camp meetings, brush arbors, rough-hewn meetinghouses, or even Gothic cathedrals, there were altars. Before there were handsome formal churches, and before evangelicals equipped their buildings with theater seats, huge platforms, and state-of-the-art sound systems, the altar was already of utmost importance to people who wanted an encounter with God.

There were public invitations before Billy Graham, Billy Sunday, Dwight Moody, Charles Finney, Francis Asbury, the Wesley brothers, George Whitefield, or Jonathan Edwards.

There were altars before Arminius, Calvin, Luther, and Augustine focused their spiritual energies on free will, the sovereignty of God, the inspiration of the Scriptures, the priesthood of believers, and the authority of the church. And regardless of cultural backgrounds and theological conclusions, faith has been proclaimed for thousands of years to spiritually concerned people who sought places for an encounter with God. For great hosts of people, these encounters have been at altars of prayer.

Giants of the faith have always believed there were special times and places where concerned men could meet God. Pious men of faith have always persuaded others to find a place where God meets both sinners and believers.

No altar of wood, stone, or precious metals has ever in itself contained the presence of God. When the children of Israel tried to accommodate the presence of God to a gold-encrusted box that their troops could carry into battle, they became vulnerable to complete demoralization when the box was ultimately captured and disappeared. Idolizing an altar may be as spiritually debilitating as idolizing anything else. But having an altar is a sacred reminder of the times and places of our special encounters with God.

Each altar experience in Bible times has its present-day message. The altar is as rich in its symbolic meaning as it is in its religious heritage. Wherever the mind, emotions, and will of man submit in obedience to the sovereign will of God, the place of this encounter becomes an altar. Marking spiritual sites with a formation of stones, building a beautiful center of worship, or making provision for a backless bench as a convenient place for prayer during public worship at the conclusion of the sermon is a matter of tradition, convenience, and architectural style. Even the unique holiness tables in Salvation Army citadels around the world are a convenient, symbolic, and visible aid to seeking God for sanctifying grace. What then is the significance of an altar experience?

Pagan Altars

One of the most famous altars in the ancient world was pagan. It sat on the brow of a hill overlooking the city of Pergamum, some 15 miles inland from the Aegean Sea in Turkey, or Asia Minor as it was called in Bible times. This ancient city, which supported a library of no less than 200,000 scrolls, second only to Alexandria in the entire world, was known, however, as the seat of Satan.

According to William Barclay, this tag, the seat of Satan, was given Pergamum by John in the Book of Revelation for two possible reasons: (1) Pergamum was the regional center for the Romans, who administered the law of Caesar worship. Here a man was required under threat of death to take the name Lord and ascribe it to Caesar, not Christ. (2) And here in Pergamum was the famous altar to Zeus, built in memory of a great victory against the Gauls in 240 B.C. The altar to Zeus was erected 800 feet up on Pergamum's conical hill. The altar itself was 40 feet high, situated on a projection of rock that made the altar look exactly like a huge throne. Smoke from the sacrifices to Zeus could be seen all day long from all over the city below.

This altar to Zeus was discovered in 1871 by Germans who dismantled it for the voyage through the Aegean and Mediterranean seas, past Gibraltar, and through the North Atlantic, where it was eventually reconstructed and may be seen today in an East Berlin museum.

Archaeologists have uncovered many altars in pre-Hebrew Palestine, all the way from the small temple in Ai to the large, 28-feet-square altar at Megiddo that served as a model for James Michener in *The Source*.

The Mosaic code took over the idea of an altar, cleansed it, purified it, and adapted it to God's purposes. The pagan altar was taken over by the Hebrews and sanctified as a centerpiece of Old Testament worship. The altar became the place of spiritual renewal through prayer, praise, sacrifice, and commitment.

The first altar mentioned in the Bible came from the hands of Noah just after he brought his family out of the ark. Noah's altar was a symbol of gratitude and promise:

> Then Noah built an altar
> and sacrificed . . . some of the animals and birds
>
> . . .
>
> Jehovah was pleased with the sacrifice
> and said to himself,
> ". . . I will never again curse the earth
>
> . . .
>
> As long as the earth remains,
> there will be springtime and harvest,
> cold and heat, winter and summer,
> day and night."
> *Gen. 8:20-22, TLB*

Abraham and His Family

There is comfort in the sentiment that says, "Surely the Lord is in this place" (Gen. 28:16, NIV). It is important to us that God's presence seems to be in some places more than others. Identifying the presence of God with a geographic spot strikes a deep chord in the human spirit. Places where we have watched beautiful sunsets, places where lovers have made promises to each other, places where an idea struck, fields of victory, mountains of achievement, and places of deep relaxation and peace are only a few of the geographic locations that add emotional meaning to our lives. But nothing is more significant in our spiritual pilgrimages than the places where God has met with us.

With the exception of his moral compromise in Egypt, Abraham's entire spiritual sojourn can be traced by the altars he built. When he was 75 years old, Abraham broke the continuity of his life and set out for Canaan with his wife, Sarah, his nephew, Lot, and all the extended family, plus their great flocks of sheep and herds of cattle. With all of his possessions in hand, Abraham traveled into the heart of Canaan to a great landmark tree at Shechem. Here, surrounded by the threats and intimidations of the local residents, God said: "To your offspring I will give this land" (Gen. 12:7, NIV). And, in commemoration of God's promise, Abraham built an altar.

> Then Jehovah appeared to Abram and said,
> "I am going to give this land to your descendants."
> And Abram built an altar there
> to commemorate Jehovah's visit.
> *Gen. 12:7, TLB*

This was an altar of gratitude. Is there any follower of Jesus who has not occasioned a need to express gratitude at an altar? Abraham built his altar of stone, and we build ours of wood; but the idea of gratitude is the same, then and now. After building the altar of gratitude at Shechem, Abram traveled on south where he continued to build altars.

> Afterwards Abram left that place
> and traveled southward to the hilly country
>
> . . .
>
> There he made camp.
> *Gen. 12:8, TLB*

From the campsite in the hills, Abraham journeyed on farther south, pitching his tent between Bethel on the west and Ai on the east. And here he built another altar:

> . . . and made an altar to the Lord
> and prayed to him.
> Thus he continued slowly southward
> to the Negeb,
> pausing frequently.
> *Gen. 12:8-9, TLB*

The most severe spiritual test Abraham ever suffered was the command to offer his son Isaac in sacrifice. The God who had said, "Through Isaac shall your descendants be named" (Gen. 21:12, RSV), now said, "Take your son . . . and offer him . . . as a burnt offering" (22:2, RSV).

This was the altar of contradiction. Does it ever seem to you that God is not consistent? Has He ever promised to remove a mountain and didn't? Has He ever given you a son and then taken him away to a mission field for a life of sacrifice or allowed him to die in a senseless war? If you have ever been to the altar of contradiction, you know something of Abraham's feeling when he "rose early in the morning, . . . and saw the place afar off" (Gen. 22:3-4, RSV).

God tested Abraham's [faith and obedience]
. . .
When they arrived at the place where God had told
Abraham to go,
he built an altar . . . ready for the fire,
and then tied Isaac
and laid him on the altar over the wood.

. . .
Then Abraham noticed a ram caught by its horns in a bush.
So he took the ram and sacrificed it,
instead of his son . . .
Abraham named the place
"Jehovah provides"—
and it still goes by that name to this day.
Gen. 22:1, 9, 13-14, TLB

Like father, like son. After watching his father, Abraham, build altars through all of his own growing-up years, Isaac also marked his own spiritual pilgrimage by altars.

When he went to Beer-sheba,
Jehovah appeared to him on the night of his arrival.
"I am the God of Abraham your father," he said.
"Fear not, for I am with you
and will bless you,
and will give you so many descendants
that they will become a great nation
. . ."
Then Isaac built an altar and worshiped Jehovah;
and he settled there,
and his servants dug a well.
Gen. 26:23-25, TLB

In the passing of years the third generation of altar builders in Abraham's family did their work. Jacob and Esau had their fiasco over an inheritance and exchanged a bowl of pottage. Jacob won. But in winning, he lost. Isaac was deceived. Esau was angry. Jacob was afraid. And Isaac's wife knew she had manipulated the family one time too many.

But the day of truth finally came. Jacob had to face Esau. Jacob was overcome with fear when he saw Esau coming with 400 men. He thought his day as the winner in a family feud was over, and Esau's day of revenge would begin. But when they faced each other, Esau drew a smile instead of a sword. They embraced, met each other's families, and took steps to live again as brothers. The cheated had forgiven the cheater. Out of sheer joy and gratitude, Jacob built an altar at Shechem and then at Bethel (Gen. 33:18-20; 35:5-7).

The spiritual heritage of altar building had been successfully handed down through the generations of Abraham. And it was time now for God to lead Moses in systematizing this spiritual impulse of man to identify the place and the times when God meets His people in sacred encounters.

The Altars of Moses

Have you ever been badgered by people who wouldn't leave you alone even when you intended them no harm? That is what Moses faced with the Amalekites. Moses and his people meant no harm. They were only passing through the land. But the Amalekites didn't like their presence and proposed to stop them with violence. After a marvelous story of Moses holding up his hands toward God, even when his arms were so weary Aaron and Hur had to support him, the Israelites won the battle, and the Amalekites fled in disarray. This called for the building of an altar of victory:

> Moses built an altar
> and called it
> The Lord is my Banner.
> *Exod. 17:15, NIV*

In the same chapter of Exodus that contains the Ten Commandments, God also gave Moses the instructions for building an altar.

> The altars you make for me
> must be simple altars
> . . .
> and I will come and bless you there.
> . . .
> use only uncut stones . . .
> Don't chip or shape the stones with a tool,
> for that would make them unfit for my altar.
> And don't make steps for the altar,
> or someone might look up
> beneath the skirts of your clothing
> and see your nakedness.
> *Exod. 20:24-26, TLB*

Early on, during his conquest of Canaan, Joshua built an altar of commitment. He built it just as God had directed Moses, with uncut stones on which no tool had been laid. And as the people watched, Joshua copied each of the Ten Commandments as a covenant renewal. And there before this altar, while the men held the ark of the covenant, Joshua "read all the words of the law," omitting none.

The Altars of the Judges and Prophets

The sojourn of the altar in the Old Testament keeps on rolling through religious history. While Gideon hid out in a secret threshing floor to avoid the Midianites, who had terrorized his land for seven years, the Lord appeared and called him out to lead the people back to righteousness. After some discussion about the poor image he had of himself, Gideon accepted the assignment from the Lord. For starters he pulled down the altar to Baal, which had been a community center during the years of occupation. But even before his night raid on the pagan altar,

> Gideon built an altar there
> and named it
> "The Altar of Peace."
> *Judg. 6:24, TLB*

For most Christians, marriage at the altar of the church is important. But after a terrifying experience with the Benjaminites, the men of Israel swore an oath against any of their daughters ever marrying men from the camps of that tribe. It seems like a strange reason for building an altar, but Israel was making a new commitment. The Scripture says,

> The next morning they were up early
> and built an altar.
> *Judg. 21:4, TLB*

The good and godly man, Samuel, who served Israel as prophet, priest, and judge, was also a man of the altar. The *New International Version* tells the story beautifully:

> Samuel continued as judge over Israel
> all the days of his life.
> From year to year he went on a circuit
> from Bethel to Gilgal to Mizpah,
> judging Israel in all those places.
> But he always went back to Ramah,
> where his home was,
> and there he also judged Israel.
> And he built an altar there to the Lord.
> *1 Sam. 7:15-17*

Saul, who was not distinguished for his piety, continued the Hebrew tradition of altar building after his victory at Michmash (1 Sam. 14:35).

But it was left to the great King David to lift the spiritual level of the people in preparation for building the permanent Temple. When David became king, the first thing he did was to bring the ark of the covenant to Jerusalem, after a sojourn of 20 years in the countryside. David called the people away from the fertility gods of the pagans, all the time seeking the mind of God on where the Temple should be built.

Under the leading of the Lord, David sought out a piece of hilltop real estate owned by a farmer, Ornan, sometimes called Araunah (2 Samuel 24). When the farmer saw the king and his entourage coming, he left his work on the threshing floor and "bowed to the ground before King David."

David said to Ornan,
"Let me buy this threshing-floor from you
at its full price;
then I will build an altar to the Lord
. . ."

"Take it, my lord, and use it as you wish,"
Ornan said to David. . . .
"No," the king replied

. . .

"I will not offer a burnt offering that has cost me nothing!"
So David paid Ornan $4,300 in gold,
and built an altar to the Lord.
1 Chron. 21:22-26, TLB

This is the altar of personal responsibility. In another record of this same story, David responded to the free offer of land and sacrificial animals by saying to Araunah, "I will not sacrifice to the Lord my God . . . offerings that cost me nothing" (2 Sam. 24:24, NIV).

The Hebrew tradition of building altars reached its grandest moment in the building of the Temple when two altars became the centerpieces of the construction and in the worship of the faithful.

In the outer court of the Temple was a huge altar, 15 feet high and 30 feet long, facing the east entrance. Here it stood for 300 years as a first reminder to the entering worshipers that sacrifices for sin must be made first when coming to God.

God also commanded Moses to build an altar of incense, sometimes called the golden altar. Incense was burned on this second altar morning and evening, symbolizing the prayers of the people wafted up toward God. This is the altar where Zacharias was officiating when he was visited by the angels who told him:

Your wife Elizabeth will bear you a son!
And you are to name him John.
Luke 1:13, TLB

However, from Noah, through Abraham, Moses, and all of the spiritual leaders of the Old Testament, the prayers and sacrifices associated with worship at the altar were never superficial acts of ritual. Man had a need to focus on specific places where God was known to meet His people. For all these Hebrew leaders, the place of spiritual encounter was the altar. The altar symbolized man's encounter with God.

Our church altar, which serves today as a convenient kneeling place, is not unrelated to the elaborate altars of the Hebrew people in the Temple. We feel we are more likely to meet God at the public altar than any other place in our church. Some of us have places of prayer in our homes that have become altars for spiritual encounter. But like Noah, we turn in gratitude to the altar. Or like Abraham, many of us can mark the important points in our sojourn by spiritual encounters at the altar. Like Moses, the altar for many of us is a place of covenant, or like Joshua, a visible reminder of who we are and what God has done for us. Like Isaac, some of us have been to our own Moriah. The saddest day in Jerusalem came when the pagan Antiochus Epiphanes carried off the golden altar in 169 B.C. And the abomination of desolation came two years later when he replaced it with a statue of Zeus.

And it is a sad day in any of our churches when we allow anyone to take away the significance of the altar as the place where we commonly expect God to meet us on a personal basis. And it will be an abomination, and the beginning of a time of spiritual desolation, if the altar is ever replaced with a substitute, however beautiful or sublime.

The New Testament Altar

Everything the system of altars and animal sacrifices stood for in the Tabernacle, and later in the Temple, came to an impressive and dramatic peak once annually on the Day of Atonement. This great religious event came each year on the 10th day of the 7th month. It was regulated by well-structured procedures. All work ceased. Children were dismissed from school. Everyone fasted. Then at the appointed time they all gathered in the Tabernacle and later in the Temple for the greatest religious ceremony of the entire year.

Three big moments characterized the events of the day. First, each person offered up sacrifices for their own sins at the huge bronze altar just inside the Temple entrance. A rich man was expected to bring a heifer, while a poor man could offer two pigeons or turtledoves. But the great middle class of worshipers brought a lamb for sacrifice, a lamb without blemish. The throat of the heifer, the bird, or the lamb was cut; and the blood, which was caught in a pan, was sprinkled on the horns of the altar. During all this ritual, the priests were standing by, praying for the sins of the people, while the people were praying for themselves.

The second big spiritual event on the Day of Atonement was the sacrifice done by the high priest for himself and for all the other priests. Two male goats were brought to the altar, where one was slain and its blood spread on the altar. The second goat was taken out beyond the city wall where a ceremony took place. While the people mocked and taunted the vulnerable goat, the priest ceremoniously placed on the animal's head all the sins of the people. Then this animal, which had become the scapegoat, was driven out into the desert, rejected and despised, to carry on himself all the sins of the people.

And finally, the most important event of the day came when the high priest entered the holy of holies and came before the mercy seat on top of the ark of the covenant. This ark, which was about the same size as a man's casket, was overlaid with gold on the inside and out, complete with a decorative rim of pure gold on all sides. Four golden rings complete with staves equipped the ark for travel. On each end, as symbolic protectors, were two cherubim, also in gold. Inside the ark were sacred objects such as the Ten Commandments, a pot of manna, and Aaron's rod.

Situated just behind the golden altar was the holy of

holies, the most sacred spot on earth. Only the high priest ever went inside this holy place, and even he was safeguarded by cords attached to his ankles for retrieving his body in case of an inopportune death. Here at the mercy seat the priest prayed again for the sins of the people.

In these events on the annual Day of Atonement we have the raw materials of a New Testament theology of the altar. (1) The sacrificial lamb of the Old Testament was a type of the ultimate sacrifice, the Lamb of God who took away the sin of the world. (2) Christ became the ultimate scapegoat on whose head the sins of the people were placed. He was rejected and despised as He suffered outside the gate of Jerusalem, crucified between rogues. And (3), the exclusive nature of the holy of holies was destroyed forever when the veil was torn from top to bottom at the moment Christ died. This is why the last prophet, John the Baptist, turned to the people when he saw Jesus coming and said, "Behold the Lamb of God, which taketh away the sin of the world" (John 1:29). This is why John spoke of the Lamb of God who was slain from the foundation of the world (Rev. 13:8). And this is why John said, "If we walk in the light as He is in the light, we have fellowship with one another, and the blood of Jesus Christ His Son cleanses us from all sin" (1 John 1:7, NKJV).

Christ fulfilled the system of altars and sacrifices. He is our living Altar. Incense and animal blood are outdated as means of divine forgiveness and spiritual communion. Smoke in our eyes and the sounds and smells of dying animals in our ears and nostrils have given over to the majesty of a Savior, who loves us when we don't deserve it, who forgives us when we have done nothing to earn forgiveness, who fills us with His presence when we would otherwise be empty and spiritually bankrupt. This is why we gather in our churches and sing:

>Redeemed—how I love to proclaim it!
>Redeemed by the blood of the Lamb!
>Redeemed through His infinite mercy,
>His child, and forever, I am.

And finally, the writer of Hebrews sums up the New Testament theology of the altar: "Neither by the blood of goats and calves, but by his own blood he entered in once into the holy place, having obtained eternal redemption for us" (Heb. 9:12). The Christian altar is Christ, our Lord.

3

Heaven's Golden Altar

IF HEAVEN is a real place with real people—and I believe it is—we who enter its golden gates are going to experience a praise and worship service beyond anything our earthbound minds can now imagine. According to John's vision, the spiritual setting for this service will be the shores of the sea of glass, before the heavenly throne, under the canopy of a beautiful rainbow, in the presence of the golden altar. Surrounding the throne will be a 24-voice choir clothed in white and adorned with crowns of gold.

The Bible gives no indication of band or orchestra music during this great worship gathering. But there will be flashes of lightning and peals of thunder enough to capture the imagination.

Directly before the heavenly throne will be seven blazing lamps whose flaming images will be reflected in the crystal-clear sea of glass. And as the service opens, heavenly creatures will repeat a chorus over and over again:

> "Holy, holy, holy
> is the Lord God Almighty,
> who was, and is, and is to come."
> *Rev. 4:8, NIV*

There will be a moment of high pageantry when the 24 elders kneel before the throne, lift their crowns, and leave them before the throne. In response to this combined act of adoration, a great chorus will sing a heavenly anthem.

> "You are worthy, our Lord and God,
> to receive glory and honor and power,
> for you created all things,
> and by your will they were created
> and have their being."
> *Rev. 4:11, NIV*

As John continued to visualize this service from the confines of his cave on Patmos—since there was no possible way he could go to church that Sunday—he saw a mighty angel holding a scroll with words on both sides of a parchment secured with seven seals. John saw the angel as he made a proclamation in the form of a question:

> "Who is worthy
> to break the seals
> and
> open the scroll?"
> *Rev. 5:2, NIV*

John wept at the lack of positive response to the question: "No one in heaven or on earth or under the earth could open the scroll" (v. 3, NIV). Even the edges of the scroll could not be pulled back for a partial glimpse at its message.

But suddenly, the heavenly service, as John saw it, moved toward a dramatic climax as the Lamb of God, who had been slain from the foundation of the world, stood in the center of the throne, alive and well, reaching out to receive the scroll with its seven seals from the angel who held it. At this moment the service of praise and worship exploded in ecstasy beyond itself. The choir, each with a harp and each with a golden bowl containing the prayers of the saints, began a new song:

> "You are worthy to take the scroll
> and to open its seals,
> because you were slain,
> and with your blood you purchased men for God
> from every tribe and language and people and nation.

. . .
And they will reign on the earth."
Rev. 5:9-10, NIV

As though the heavenly setting, glorious singing, and the appearance of the Lord were not enough, John watched as more than 100 million angels encircled the throne to sing in magnificent stereophonic sound.

"Worthy is the Lamb, who was slain,
to receive power and wealth and wisdom and strength
and honor and glory and praise!"
Rev. 5:12, NIV

Inspired and infused with rapturous joy, every creature —and that means, totally, all creation—joined in the refrain in heaven, on earth, and under the earth:

"To him who sits on the throne
and to the Lamb
be praise and honor and glory and power,
for ever and ever!"
Rev. 5:13, NIV

As a fitting end to this heavenly extravaganza of music and worship, a quartet closed the universal adoration with a solemn "Amen." (What John did not see was the day on earth when George Frideric Handel would set the words of the heavenly choir to music in the immortal *Messiah.*)

After the music had ended, after the lightning and thunder had died down, and after Christ the Sacrificial Lamb had opened the seven seals, John saw something happening that should cheer the heart of us all who are still on our pilgrimage.

As John turned his fascination away from the throne to the sea of glass, he became aware of a numberless throng of people from "every nation, tribe, people and language" who had arrived to join the worshipers "before the throne" (Rev. 7:9, NIV).

They were wearing white—the official color of heaven —and were waving palm branches as they walked. John makes no mention of the contrast among green palm branches, white robes, and blue sky—there was no night there—but the sight must have been overwhelmingly beautiful.

These multitudes, lately arrived, also struck out in their songs of praise. And when they had finished, one of the elders asked John:

"Who are they, and where did they come from?"
Rev. 7:13, NIV

With all heavenly respect, John replied:

"Sir, you know."

And John was right, for the elder replied:

"These are they who have come out of the great tribulation;
they have washed their robes and made them white
in the blood of the Lamb."
Rev. 7:14, NIV

*   *   *

The thought of a numberless throng marching into heaven brings me back to the days of my childhood in Springfield, Ill. As a matter of habit I made a trip to the city library, usually once a week, to return and borrow books. I don't know how I got started with this regimen. The books were not assigned by the teacher and, more often than not, were unrelated to my schoolwork. I guess I was just fortunate in having a teacher who taught me not only how to read but also how to enjoy it.

But that is not the point. Since I had no bicycle until I was in the eighth grade, most of these treks were on foot. And that was all right, too, because there was more to see and absorb on foot than could have been taken in on a bicycle or in a car.

There were two houses we (I was usually in the company of one or two other boys) often passed because we planned it that way. We went out of our way to pass the home of Abraham Lincoln, where we could stand across the street and fantasize about him coming out the front door. And the other house we often walked by was the home of the poet Vachel Lindsay, located on the corner just south of the governor's mansion.

Mr. Lindsay died about the time I was in the third or fourth grade at Hay-Edwards School. But all of us in our grade school English classes taught by Miss Barnes were familiar with at least two of his poems, "Abraham Lincoln Walks at Midnight" and "General William Booth Enters into Heaven." Most of us memorized parts of these poems, and a few memorized them both.

But it is the poem about General Booth entering heaven that relates to John's vision of the great worship service in heaven.

When General Booth was dying, it seems the word went out to his converts and followers all over the world. Suddenly, as if by some kind of magic, they began to gather themselves along the Thames River around the International Headquarters of the Salvation Army, just below St. Paul's Cathedral in London.

By the time official word was received that General Booth was dead, they were there by the thousands, ready to begin their march to heaven with their beloved general. Vachel Lindsay's poem is about these people and this march by the unnumbered thousands who joined him on the way. They were ready because they had been to Jesus and were washed in the blood of the Lamb.

In more recent years, two Salvation Army officers have written, and then produced, a powerful and gripping musical based on Mr. Lindsay's poem. When the musical was presented in the Civic Auditorium in Kansas City, the doors were locked against the overflow crowd outside, and no one was allowed to enter or leave during the presentation. The emotional impact of the performances was deep and memorable.

In the musical, the Salvationists, accompanied by their best brass and drums, sang with great power and feeling about "the hoodlum, and the hooker, and the hobo" who were in that crowd marching to heaven. They sang about "the drunkard, and the drug addict, and the dropout," for they were also there. They sang about the streetwalker who all but owned 100 yards of the Strand as her personal property. But she, like all the others, joined the march of those "washed in the blood of the Lamb."

In his version of General Booth's march to heaven, Vachel Lindsay described these Blood-washed social rejects who marched as "vermin-eaten saints with moldy breath; unwashed legions with the ways of death."

But these legions John saw gathering around the sea of glass from every nation and tongue and the moldy multitude whom Vachel Lindsay saw marching to heaven with General Booth will one day become reality for all of us who are washed in the blood of the Lamb.

There will come a time when the last sermon has been preached and the last hymn has been sung and the final prayer has been made. There will come a day when it's time for us to begin the last lap of our march to heaven. With faces set toward the welcome smiles of those who wait to receive us, we will become members of the congregation in that great service of praise and worship before the throne of Christ the Lamb.

* * *

But now, let's pause for a moment. We have been talking about the most important Person in heaven, Christ the Lamb of God. Now I wish we could think about the most important piece of furniture in heaven, the golden altar.

Most of us think about altars in evangelical meetinghouses where people kneel to pray, or altars that are the centers of worship in Roman Catholic and Anglican churches. But in heaven, between the throne and the sea of glass, is a golden altar. And in John's vision from Patmos, this altar played a significant role in the worship service.

Altars are mentioned hundreds of times in the Bible, but the most significant symbolisms on the altar are in the Book of Revelation. Even a superficial reading of this book, which is rich in spiritual imagery, cannot help but make us aware that in heaven the altar is a very important piece of celestial furniture.

There is no need for long elaboration, and the idea of the altar in heaven can't be pushed too far in its application on earth. But the golden altar in heaven is important, and helpful in understanding the place and the meaning of altars in the Bible. There are five faithful references to the altar in John's Revelation that may also be applied to altar encounters on earth.

*   *   *

1. The altar in heaven and on earth is a place of eternal safety and protection.

> I saw under the altar
> the souls of those who had been slain
> because of the word of God
> and the testimony they had maintained.
> *Rev. 6:9, NIV*

God does not settle all wrongs the moment they occur, maybe not for years, if ever in this life. But the altar is the place where all injustice and personal wrongs may be taken and left in God's care. And according to the Scripture, He has an altar where these matters are kept and not forgotten. In the resurrection morning, God has a special place for those who have left the settlement of unfair treatment and personal abuse to His ultimate care.

We most often think of altars in our evangelical churches as the place we go to pray for salvation. But altar prayers can be for many other reasons. Can you imagine what spiritual tide might rise in any church where everyone who is suffering over injustices could take these dark memories to God's altar and leave them there. When we strive to settle the issues of injustice in our lives by our own strategies, we more often generate reciprocating injustice. But when we are able to leave our injustices in God's hands, His solutions ultimately turn out best.

*   *   *

2. The altar in heaven and on earth is the place where the prayers of believers touch the will and purposes of God.

> Another angel, . . . came and stood at the altar.
> He was given much incense
> to offer, with the prayers of all the saints,
> on the
> golden altar before the throne.
>   . . .
>
> Then the angel took the censer,
> filled it with fire from the altar,
> and hurled it on the earth;
> and there came peals of thunder,
> rumblings, flashes of lightning
> and an earthquake.
> *Rev. 8:3, 5, NIV*

Praying believers never seem to be afraid of the altar. The altar is more than a convenient place to kneel at appropriate times. The altar is a place where believers meet God, encounter themselves, voice their praises, and think about their needs. The results of these prayers are then in God's hands. Quiet prayers are like incense and are not more or less important than prayers that shake things up like an earthquake. A prayer is a prayer in God's scheme of things.

It is encouraging to notice that the angel did not select out certain prayers of quality, properly ordered. At heaven's altar there is a response to all prayers. The altar in the humblest meetinghouse, the kneeling rail in the most sophisticated church or most awe-inspiring cathedral, and all similar places in between are all in their own ways earthly counterparts of the golden altar in heaven.

Neither is there profit in vaulted language. God is not interested in how we articulate our prayers at the altar but in how we feel about ourselves while we are praying. Jesus made short shrift of the haughty man who thanked God he was not as other men, particularly the man of low reputation who beat his breast and remained some distance away. The prayer that was heard in heaven was short but from the heart: "God, have mercy on me, a sinner" (Luke 18:13, NIV). There was no doubt about which man went home justified.

*   *   *

3. The altar in heaven, and on earth, is a place of personal refuge:

> I heard a voice
> coming from the horns
> of the
> golden altar
> that is before God.
> *Rev. 9:13, NIV*

In the Old Testament theology of the altar, the horns on the four corners of the altar were always places of protection for people who were in danger from their adversaries. If the person in danger could make it to the altar, he was safe because the horns were considered off limits to violence.

When Solomon's appointment as king was announced, his chief rival, Adonijah, was in immediate danger. It was customary for ancient kings on accession to eliminate their competition, a tradition with its counterpart in modern times.

Adonijah, on hearing the news of Solomon's kingship, immediately fled to the sanctuary and touched the horns of the altar. The biblical account is recorded in 1 Kings:

> At this, all Adonijah's guests rose in alarm and dispersed.
> But Adonijah, in fear of Solomon,
> went and took hold of
> the horns of the altar. . . .
> "He says, 'Let King Solomon swear to me today
> that he will not put his servant to death with the sword.'"
> Solomon replied,
> "If he shows himself to be a worthy man,
> not a hair of his head will fall to the ground . . ."
> Then . . . they brought him down from the altar.
> *1 Kings 1:49-53, NIV*

There was something about those four projections on the four corners of the altar that made time stand still. While the fugitive or the fearful held to the horns of the altar, they were safe. This provided time to think, to negotiate, and to plan. This time at the altar gave the fugitive an opportunity to listen for God's direction.

This idea of the altar as a place for temporary protection, where harm and hate were excluded, kept the oppressed from the oppressor. Obviously, no one can take up residence at the mourner's bench in our churches. But for each of us, the altar can become a place of temporary respite from the battles of life. Providing refuge during times of crisis is one of the sacred functions of the altar.

*   *   *

4. The altar in heaven and on earth is clearly identified as a vital part of the Temple of God.

> I was given a reed like a measuring rod
> and was told, "Go and measure the temple of God
> and the altar,
> and count the worshipers there."
> *Rev. 11:1, NIV*

The Temple, the altar, and the worshipers are all important to each other. But the Temple and the altar are inseparably welded together. The Temple is built for the altar, and the altar is built for the Temple. Certainly the altar was never an afterthought in worship. Long before there were sanctuaries and Tabernacles, there were altars. When the Hebrew exiles came back to Jerusalem after 70 years absence—two generations—they rebuilt the altar before they rebuilt the Temple. And the dedication of the altar was tantamount to dedicating the Temple. First came the altar, then the Temple.

I have never been able to understand why any local congregation or denomination has wanted to eliminate their altar as a place for spiritual encounter. I know some have argued that it is better to pray with seekers in an inquiry room than at a public altar. However, I doubt if spiritual counseling in a closed room is any more effective than praying with a kneeling penitent at a public altar.

Dwight Moody did not use an altar in favor of an inquiry room because he felt that the latter is more private and more conducive to spiritual work. That may be true, though I doubt it. But providing seekers with a convenient place to pray is only one function of the sacred altar. The altar is an inherent part of the place where God's people gather to worship. There is no substitute for the altar as a place for encountering God.

There is a special meaning in God's request for John to measure the Temple and the altar and then count the number in the congregation. Measuring denotes a testing on God's part to see if the people are up to standard. John was using the earthly Temple and its altar as a symbol of God's altar in heaven where those who measure up as true worshipers abide with Him. John's measuring assignment reminds us of the important function of the altar as a place for self-examination and spiritual heart-searching.

* * *

5. The altar in heaven and on earth is a place of spiritual struggle and judgment.

> Another angel, who had charge of the fire,
> came from the altar
> and called in a loud voice . . . ,
> "Take your sharp sickle and gather the clusters of grapes
> from the earth's vine,
> because its grapes are ripe."
> The angel swung his sickle on the earth,
> gathered its grapes and threw them into the great winepress
> of God's wrath.
> *Rev. 14:18-19, NIV*

The signs and symbols of the altar in Revelation climax with this final picture of the victorious Christ. He is now the Reaper sent to gather the grapes of God's wrath in final judgment.

We have here the reminder that all life is determined by spiritual conflict. God sent His Son as the ultimate Sacrifice for salvation. But our struggle is for godly repentance and the human willingness to let the Lord be Lord of our lives.

Through His sacrifice we are saved from wrath and purified in holiness.

We need to remind ourselves that all the spiritual struggle that goes into living our faith is only a small suggestion of the greater struggle between heaven and hell, between God and Satan.

On earth there is nothing wrong with spiritual struggle, only in giving up. The church altar may be our place of spiritual struggle, but within ourselves we decide whether the altar will be our place of spiritual victory or defeat.

> Then I heard a loud voice from the temple saying . . .
> "Go, pour out the seven bowls of God's wrath
> on the earth."
>
> . . .
>
> And I heard the altar respond:
> "Yes, Lord God Almighty,
> True and just are your judgments."
> *Rev. 16:1, 7, NIV*

* * *

This book is about the importance of the altar and its meaning in our churches. It is also about the kinds of Christian persuasion the altar calls for.

It is no accident that the pulpit is behind the Communion table, which is behind the altar in most of our churches. These three important pieces of church furniture need to be aligned with each other symbolically and theologically.

In this chapter we have shared John's vision of the ultimate service of worship in heaven where Christ shall reign supreme. And second, we have examined the meaning of the golden altar in heaven and what it may symbolize on earth. In the next chapter we will turn to the idea of Christian persuasion in the New Testament Church. The nature and the meaning of the sacred altars in our churches depend on the persuasion that accompanies our proclamation of the gospel.

4

New Testament Persuasion

LONG AGO, during my more impressionable years, I attended a banquet in the old Astor Hotel on Times Square in New York City. It was a banquet of 650 Christian businessmen in New York. I was an immediate graduate from college, wide-eyed in the big city, and eager to learn.

I had never been in a stylish dining room like the Grand Ballroom of the Astor. As a young preacher, I was impressed with everything including the waiters, who made me feel inadequate in their long-tailed coats and striped trousers, to say nothing of their foreign accents. The overpowering chandeliers in this high-ceilinged room twinkled and sparkled more than any chandeliers I had ever seen.

The 10 men seated at each of the circular tables were self-assured, white-collar workers from Manhattan's midtown offices. Although we were served a bountiful meal, I was too impressed to eat. However, I do remember mistaking the fish course for the main dish. When they darkened the room and brought in the flaming desserts, it was like the Fourth of July. I wanted to cheer. One thing was sure: My mother never served a dinner like that in her whole life.

When the program began, I was more comfortable than I had been during the meal but was still overwhelmed. The Percy Crawford Quartet, a very famous singing group in that day, was there along with George Beverly Shea, who later became famous as soloist in the Billy Graham team. And there were three 10-minute sermons, daringly announced as 10-minute sermons. I thought this really put the speakers on the spot. And it did. But each man kept within his 10 minutes. It seemed like the congregational singing of "All Hail the Power of Jesus' Name" rocked the chandeliers.

But the life-changing moment in the total experience came for me when three men were asked to give testimonies. One was the warden of Sing Sing Prison, while the second was a distinguished-looking man introduced as a Philadelphia lawyer. And last was Mr. Swanson, president of the Thomas Baking Company, whose delivery trucks could be seen in towns from Boston to Baltimore.

Mr. Swanson told how he was converted in an "old-fashioned revival," where he knelt at a mourner's bench and "prayed through." He told how he and his wife started out in the bakery business, staying up all night to preside over their ovens, and then with baskets of bread, cookies, and cakes, walked the streets, she on one side and he on the other, knocking on doors until all the merchandise was sold.

Mr. Swanson closed his testimony by reciting a passage of Scripture that had great meaning to him. His interest and concern in 1 Cor. 2:1-5 communicated something special to me. For there in New York on that very evening, I committed to memory Paul's premier passage on preaching and took those verses to be the lifelong goal of my ministry. As a Christian university president, I travel widely, speaking to many kinds of gatherings. But there have been few times that I have failed to make my first words in a new pulpit to be a repeat of what Paul said as he looked back on the times he preached to the people of Corinth.

Paul's self-disclosure on the nature of preaching was included in a letter to a church he knew well. And in this passage, he reminded them of the kind of preaching they had heard from him when he was their spiritual leader:

And I, brethren, when I came to you,
came not with excellency of speech or of wisdom,
declaring unto you the testimony of God.
For I determined not to know any thing among you,
save Jesus Christ, and him crucified.
And I was with you in weakness, and in fear, and in much
trembling.
And my speech and my preaching
was not with enticing words of man's wisdom,
but in demonstration of the Spirit and of power:
that your faith should not stand in the wisdom of men,
but in the power of God.
1 Cor. 2:1-5

The Persuasion of Paul

Paul had a strong commitment to preaching as a major means of Christian persuasion. He did not talk about "sharing" the gospel. He preached the gospel. He proclaimed it. Earlier in this same Corinthian letter, Paul said, "It pleased God by the foolishness of preaching to save them that believe" (1:21).

During his stay in Ephesus, Paul "went into the synagogue and spoke boldly . . . reasoning and persuading concerning the things of the kingdom of God" (Acts 19:8, NKJV).

When the silversmiths of Ephesus were stirred against Paul, it was his persuasive preaching they could not take: "That not alone at Ephesus, but almost throughout all Asia, this Paul hath persuaded and turned away much people, saying that they be no gods, which are made with hands" (Acts 19:26).

Even the pagan King Agrippa said to Paul, "Almost thou persuadest me to be a Christian" (Acts 26:28). The king kept the tentmaker in bonds, even though he was moved by his sermon in the judgment hall. But much later, after Paul had arrived in Rome, the Jewish leaders there set a day when people could visit Paul to learn more about Christ. "And when they had appointed him a day, there came many to him into his lodging; to whom he expounded . . . the kingdom of God, persuading them concerning Jesus . . . And some believed" (Acts 28:23-24).

The big question, however, is not a matter of Paul's personal gifts of persuasion. He wrote the Ephesians that he came to them in weakness and fear. The significant question is, What gave Paul's message authority? Paul's sermons captured the attention of people everywhere he preached, whether it was in a Jewish synagogue, on the streets, or in the homes of citizens in cities across the ancient world, even in the judgment hall of a pagan king. If Paul saw preaching as foolishness and saw himself as weak and fearful, even in Ephesus where he had some of his greatest success, where did he get his message and what did he preach?

Kērygma, which is the word for preaching in the New Testament, refers to substance or preaching material and not to the delivery style of the preacher. The New Testament draws a clear line between preaching and teaching. *Didachē*, which is the New Testament word for teaching, focused on subject matter relating to (1) ethical instruction, (2) explanation or defense of the gospel, and (3) the exposition of theological doctrine. But we need to remind ourselves that it was by the *kērygma*, and not the *didachē*, that God was pleased to save those who believed. There was an element of evangelism in the *kērygma* that was not anticipated in the *didachē*.

Preaching, in the New Testament, was the proclamation of the gospel. It had the ring of a town crier in the Old World who would lift his voice with authority to proclaim a message he had been sent to give. The press secretary for the president of the United States communicates his message within guidelines the president has given him. If the press secretary gets outside his guidelines, he speaks no longer for the president but only for himself. And so it is with preaching. There is a body of knowledge that constitutes New Testament preaching as set forth by the apostles.

Paul's letters are the oldest Christian writings still in existence. Therefore, there is an important question concerning them: Just how close was Paul to the source of the gospel and what was the gospel Paul preached that had within it this strong element of Christian persuasion?

Although scholars do not agree on dates, they do agree that the beginning of Paul's ministry was not far removed in years from the crucifixion and resurrection of Jesus. His conversion was probably around A.D. 33 or 34. If Christ was crucified in the spring of A.D. 30, the memories of what happened were immediate enough for confirmation or denial by eyewitnesses.

Paul's visit to Jerusalem was probably two or three years after his conversion, and after he had spent two years in Arabia's desert country contemplating the meaning of the entire Christ event. This means his two-week stay in the home of Peter was no more than seven years after the crucifixion.

Following the Jerusalem trip, Paul was separated from the church for 14 years while he returned to his hometown of Tarsus, northwest of Syrian Antioch (not to be confused with Pisidian Antioch). According to C. H. Dodd, in his classic book *Apostolic Preaching*, Paul's Sanhedrin years before his conversion, his 2 years in Arabia, his Jerusalem visit, and his 14 years back home brought him down to the era when the first Epistles were written.

According to Dodd, the date when Paul received the fundamentals of the gospel was no more than 7 years after the death of Jesus. And no facts are strained to assume some knowledge of the gospel by Paul even earlier than the mid-30s A.D., through the preaching and stoning of Stephen. According to Dr. Dodd, Paul's "preaching derived from a stream very near the main source."

One of the problems in identifying the substance of Paul's preaching is the focus of his letters and the persons to whom they were addressed. He wrote to Christians, not unbelievers. Paul addressed his letters to people who were willing to move upstream against the mainstream of a pagan culture. He dealt with the theological and ethical questions that were important in retaining the Christian way of life.

However, Paul assumes in his letters that the readers already are familiar with the substance of the gospel as preached by the apostles including himself. Therefore, he used his letters to expound and explain the implications of the gospel he preached.

One of the clearest passages on the substance of Paul's sermons is 1 Cor. 15:1-23. Paul reminded the Corinthians of his preaching material:

> I declare unto you the gospel which I preached unto you,
> which also ye have received,
> and wherein ye stand;
> by which also ye are saved,
> if ye keep in memory what I preached unto you.
> *vv. 1-2*

Paul, like all good preachers, spoke from his own knowledge, what he had experienced, and what he believed. Altars are seldom needed in churches with pastors who preach their doubts.

> For I delivered unto you first of all
> that which I also received,
> how that Christ died for our sins
> according to the scriptures;
> and that he was buried,
> and that he rose again the third day
> according to the scriptures.
> *vv. 3-4*

After marshaling evidence on the Resurrection by those who saw the risen Lord—Peter, the Twelve, 500 brethren, James, all of the apostles, and himself—he declared his feelings of unworthiness to be numbered with the apostles; and then Paul bridged the substance of his own preaching to the preaching of the other believers.

> Therefore whether it were I or they,
> so we preach,
> and so ye believed.
> *v. 11*

Finally, in this passage, Paul talks about the futility of preaching the Crucifixion without also preaching the Resurrection. And since there was a resurrection of Christ, we may confirm our own hope in the resurrection of all believers.

> If Christ be not risen,
> then is our preaching vain,
> and your faith is also vain. . . .
> And . . . ye are yet in your sins. . . .
> If in this life only we have hope in Christ,
> we are of all men most miserable.
> *vv. 14, 17, 19*

Another strong passage that opens a window on the substance of Paul's sermons is his letter to the Romans, 10:8-15.

> The word of faith, which we preach;
> . . . if thou shalt confess . . . the Lord Jesus,
> and shalt believe in thine heart
> that God hath raised him from the dead,
> thou shalt be saved.
> *vv. 8-9*

In this passage Paul makes an issue of the gospel for everyone, Jew and Greek alike. The provisions of the gospel are universal.

> For whosoever
> shall call upon the name of the Lord
> shall be saved.
> *v. 13*

And finally, Paul makes another appeal for the importance of preaching.

> How shall they believe in him of whom
> they have not heard?
> and how shall they hear
> without a preacher?
> And how shall they preach,
> except they be sent?
> *vv. 14-15*

There is one more element in the material Paul preached that must not be forgotten, even in a high-tech age of transplants, artificial insemination, and biogenetics. Paul believed with all his heart in a final judgment where every man will be held accountable.

Why dost thou judge thy brother? . . .
we shall all stand
before the judgment seat of Christ.
Rom. 14:10

* * *

We must all appear
before the judgment seat
of Christ.
2 Cor. 5:10

* * *

In the day when
God shall judge the secrets
of men
by Jesus Christ.
Rom. 2:16

* * *

Judge nothing before the time,
until the Lord come,
who . . . will bring to light
the hidden things of darkness.
1 Cor. 4:5

In summary, Paul preached (1) the fulfillment of the prophecies according to the Scriptures, (2) the new age ushered in by the coming of Christ, (3) the death and resurrection of Jesus, (4) the exaltation of Christ at the right hand of God, (5) the return of Christ as Judge and Savior, and (6) salvation through Christ as Lord.

The Persuasion of Peter

There was an element of persuasion present throughout all the ministry of the Jerusalem church. They must have taken their pattern from Jesus, who "came into Galilee, preaching the gospel . . . and saying, The time is fulfilled . . . repent ye, and believe the gospel" (Mark 1:14-15).

Those Jerusalem believers must have caught the evangelistic significance of Christ's commission, "Go ye into all the world, and preach the gospel" (Mark 16:15).

When all their strategies for spreading the gospel got them the blunt edge of Middle East terrorism, the Jerusalem Christians just kept on preaching: "There was a great persecution against the church which was at Jerusalem; and they were all scattered abroad . . . except the apostles. . . . They that were scattered abroad went every where preaching the word" (Acts 8:1, 4).

Peter's sermon at Pentecost is another example of preaching among the Spirit-filled disciples after Pentecost. If you had heard Peter and Paul in separate revivals in Jerusalem and Antioch, it would have been obvious they were preaching from the same source. Today we would have said they had read the same book. But with Peter and Paul and the others, they had known the same Person.

If we assume that the record of Peter's sermon in Acts 2 is really an outline or summary statement of his sermon, it is easy to identify the salient points:

1. "Standing up with the eleven" (v. 14). Peter was the spokesman, but his doctrine was approved by the other disciples. The content of his message was commonly accepted.

2. "Jesus of Nazareth, a man approved of God among you" (v. 22). Everything in the new age hinged on the fact that Jesus had come. His signs and wonders were accepted as fact among the people to whom Peter preached. The life and ministry of Christ among the people is a good starting place for any sermon.

3. "Ye have taken, and by wicked hands have crucified" (v. 23). There was meaning in the crucifixion of Jesus that went beyond the fact of another violent death. In His death there was unique power. Jesus did not die for His own sins but for the sins of all the people.

4. "This Jesus hath God raised up, whereof we are all witnesses" (v. 32). The fact of the Resurrection was central in apostolic preaching. The Church was founded on the belief men had in the resurrection of Jesus. Church members would die rather than deny the risen Jesus as Lord.

5. "Therefore being by the right hand of God exalted" (v. 33). There could be no return of Christ as Judge and Lord unless He was first exalted with the Father. Although Jesus was at the right hand of God in heaven, His presence was among men on earth through the presence of the Holy Spirit.

6. "Therefore let all the house of Israel know assuredly, that God hath made that same Jesus ... both Lord and Christ" (v. 36). Christ is Lord to all who receive Him as Sovereign in the kingdom of God, the Ruler of their lives.

With the ring of authority that came from Peter's personal knowledge of Christ as Lord and from his recent experience in the Upper Room, it should not be a surprise to anyone that his message brought an evangelistic response. Peter had no kneeling altar as we know it in our Protestant churches today. For one thing, he was preaching outside, under the sky in an unannounced gathering. But he had preached for a decision. "Now when they heard this, they were pricked in their heart, and said ... what shall we do?" (v. 37).

7. Then Peter said, "Repent, and be baptized every one of you in the name of Jesus Christ for the remission of sins, and ye shall receive the gift of the Holy Ghost" (v. 38).

Here then is the first sermon and the first altar service after Pentecost. Luke's report on this response is electrifying; there was a head count of 3,000 souls, persons who repented and believed (v. 41).

In Billy Graham's introduction to Leighton Ford's book *The Christian Persuader,* he says, "If the church would return to the simple, authoritative, and urgent message of the kerygma, we could accomplish many things. . . . It was by the clear preaching of the kerygma that the early church made its converts and its impact on the Roman world."

DIVISION TWO

The Long Road Back

Why should we tarry when Jesus is pleading,
  Pleading for you and for me?
Why should we linger and heed not His mercies,
  Mercies for you and for me?
      —from the hymn "Softly and Tenderly"

5

Regaining
the Lost Estate

THE CHRISTIAN PERSUASION of Peter and Paul had scarcely become echoes before vast changes began to evolve in the church. By strategic location, numerical strength, and institutional leadership, dominance in the Christian church finally rested firmly in the Roman church. But with this shift of dominance from Jerusalem to Rome came a restructured church. As the political power of the Roman Empire began to fade, the Christian church inherited its structure, which eventually became a monolithic tower of religious power in Europe, England, and all the Mediterranean world.

When Peter and Paul preached, they extolled the name of Jesus, crucified and raised from the dead, abiding now at the right hand of God the Father. They proclaimed the gift of salvation with full forgiveness and the personal, indwelling presence of the Holy Spirit. And when they preached the gospel, they expected results. Under this kind of preaching, people came by the thousands to receive Christ as Lord. Whole areas, such as Samaria, and great cities like Ephesus were transformed through this kind of Spirit-honored preaching.

However, by the fourth century, Peter and Paul would have had a difficult time recognizing the church. As Michael Green observes in his book *Evangelism in the Church,* four major changes took place. There were radical changes in (1) the nature of faith, (2) the nature of the church, (3) the nature of church authority, and (4) the nature of worship.

Faith was transferred from the person of Christ to the church as an institution and to the sacraments that it dispensed on its own authority. Salvation came first to the church and by the church to the individual. By A.D. 250 Bishop Cyprian could say, "No man can have God for his Father who does not have the church for his mother."

Pulpits were superseded by high, gilded altars. Local pastors left their preaching ministries to become priests. The worship service was changed from a simple format to an elaborate ritual called the Mass. The gospel preaching of men like Peter and Paul was replaced with ceremony, and evangelism became a crusade to secure obedience to the church. The call to a personal faith in Christ was abandoned. There was no need in the restructured church for preaching that called nonbelievers to a verdict, unless it was a verdict in favor of the church at Rome.

This dark night of the church lasted for more than 1,000 years. The church was eventually divided between the East and the West, with loyalties focused on Constantinople or Rome. The power of the church was no longer spiritual but political. Kings and princes submitted to the authority of the church and its titular head, the pope.

*   *   *

Then came a new cultural awakening called the Renaissance. Gutenberg invented a printing press with movable type on which he printed the Bible in 1452. Michelangelo, Leonardo da Vinci, and Raphael rekindled the love of the human spirit for art. Copernicus, a contemporary of Martin Luther, challenged the minds of the people with his idea of the earth as a moving object and thereby became the father of modern astronomy. If there were any headlines in the newspapers of the 15th century, Columbus and Diaz must have had their share of banners and news reports on their explorations of a "new world." And those who wanted to think had plenty of grist for their intellectual mills supplied by the writings of Erasmus.

In the midst of these stirrings God raised up a man to lead the reform movement against the distortion of the gospel message and disintegration of spiritual leadership in the church. His name was Martin Luther.

Luther was nine years old when Columbus discovered America. And Michelangelo, Leonardo da Vinci, and Raphael were all still alive when Luther nailed his famous list of 95 questions on the door of the Castle Church in Wittenberg. Had it not been for Gutenberg's press, Luther could never have gotten the Bible to the people in their language, the vernacular of the street. Granted, Luther was not simply the product of his times. However, the traumatic changes that were shattering the cultural norms of the Middle Ages were used by the Holy Spirit in making Luther's reformations possible. For instance, the rising tide of nationalism made it possible for Luther's protector, Frederick the Wise, to stare down the authority of the Holy Roman Empire. It kept both Luther and his work alive. The church could excommunicate Luther, but they could not burn him at the stake.

As a young man, Luther was a faithful son of the Roman Catholic church. However, he became deeply troubled about the meaning of the Christian gospel. He followed the churchly route of earning God's favor by good and pious works. He joined the monastery where he could say more prayers, discipline himself more severely, fast more often, and do more acts of penance than anywhere else. But those good works only deepened the level of his spiritual anxiety and intensified its nature.

Luther's answer to the meaning of the gospel came in 1508 or 1509 while he was studying the Book of Psalms and the letters of Paul. He began to realize that salvation was not a prize to be won but a gift to be received. God's love and kindness were given to the world in the life, death, and resurrection of Jesus Christ. This undeserved and unearned gift in the finished work of Christ was the meaning of justification by faith. "The just shall live by faith" (Rom. 1:17) became a battle cry. Luther had come to recognize that justification by faith was a right and proper substitute for the Roman Catholic church's justification by the sacraments.

Besides his earthshaking doctrine of justification by faith, Luther made other contributions that helped pave the way for bringing the church back to the spirit of New Testament evangelism.

1. Luther gave the Bible back to the people. He translated the New Testament from Latin to German. For instance, he published the first edition in the fall of 1522, only one year after he was excommunicated from the church by Pope Leo X. The first edition sold out in less than three months. By 1544, the number of editions was well into the 90s, probably 95. It took 908 pages of print to contain Luther's translation of the entire Bible in 1534.

2. Luther returned music to the people. Luther published a hymnbook and encouraged congregational singing in worship services. "A Mighty Fortress Is Our God" became the great battle hymn of the Protestant Reformation. Roland Bainton, in his book *Here I Stand,* quotes Luther saying, "Experience proves that next to the Word of God, only music deserves to be extolled as the mistress and governess of the feelings of the human heart."

3. Luther returned accountability to the people and emphasized the need for every believer to be his own priest. He erased the spiritual line between the clergy and the laity by proposing the priesthood of every believer.

4. Luther further emphasized the importance of preaching and evangelism. The sermon became a major event in the worship service. The pulpit was returned to its rightful place. From Luther's time forward, great crowds have always been attracted to the men who have used their pulpits best in preaching to the needs people feel.

The evangelical church will always be in the debt of Martin Luther for being the leader who brought the church through its first giant step on the painful path back toward New Testament gospel.

* * *

John Calvin was the second great Reformer in regaining the lost estate. He laid the theological groundwork for the gospel of personal salvation.

Dr. Mendell Taylor, in *Exploring Evangelism,* gives Calvin the credit for pushing the ultimate limit of protest against the doctrine of salvation by good works in the Roman Catholic church. Calvin swung from the doctrine of good works all the way to the other end of the continuum, by teaching salvation through divinely bestowed grace without regard for man's responsibility. Dr. Taylor writes, "Out of Calvin's life and thought emerged a widespread influence based on the principle of divine grace as the only factor in man's salvation."

Calvin, who was 25 years younger than Luther, was born in France, where his father was a lawyer for the Roman Catholic church. However, Calvin's education reflected the influence of the liberal and humanistic Renaissance as known in France and particularly in the University of Paris. There is no indication that John Calvin ever became a priest. By 1533 he declared himself a Protestant. Three years later he became the leader of the Protestant pastors in Geneva.

Calvin had a brilliant mind, which he put to the task of persuasive preaching, incisive writing, and logical thinking. He was one of the chief leaders of the Reformation. His followers in France were called Huguenots. In England they were called Puritans. His major influence was in Switzerland, England, Scotland, and colonial America. He called for separation of church and state and is the first man in Europe to achieve some church independence from the state. His theology was based on five concepts that he carried out to their logical end.

1. The sovereignty of God. Like a lawyer laying out his case, everything else in Calvin's thought depended on full

recognition of this first principle, the total and absolute sovereignty of God.

2. The hopelessness of man. Total moral corruption leaves man in spiritual helplessness. He is bereft of good. He does not even have the capacity to respond to good because he is productive of every kind of evil.

3. The adequacy of Christ. In a mysterious way none of us can fully understand, the bridge between the holiness of God and the utter sinfulness of man is spanned by the sacrifice of Christ on the Cross. Christ alone could pay the price demanded to fulfill the moral law of God.

4. Salvation by grace. Man deserves nothing but damnation. His spiritual impotence is complete, and his total depravity is utterly pervasive. Therefore he can be saved from wrath only by the unmerited grace of God provided through the atonement of Christ.

5. Grace is bestowed by divine election. Mendell Taylor says, "The sovereignty of God and the bankruptcy of man become linked together in the doctrine of divine election." Thus God wills to show mercy on those who receive grace and wills to leave others destitute in the sin that bogs them down.

Many young theological students have learned the five concepts of Calvin's theology by remembering the acrostic that spells TULIP: (1) Total and absolute depravity; (2) Unconditional predestination; (3) Limited atonement; (4) Irresistible grace; and the (5) Perseverance of the saints, popularly known as "once in grace, always in grace."

The continuing influence of Calvin lingers among Protestants everywhere, but the strongest influence of Calvin may be seen most readily in Presbyterian, Baptist, Congregational, and independent "Bible" type churches. Calvin paved the way for the modern evangelical movement. He was a great leader on the long road back to New Testament gospel.

* * *

The third great Reformer who helped pave the way for the altar call was James Arminius. Martin Luther restored the great truth of justification by faith and thus broke with the Roman Catholic church, which had insisted on salvation by authority of the institution, mediated through the sacraments, and earned by spiritual merits. John Calvin restored the great truth of God's grace mediated through the sovereign will of God and the atonement of Christ as the sole means of salvation. And James Arminius focused on the free will of man to exercise faith and receive grace.

The same encyclopedia that gives considerable space to both Luther and Calvin reports of the work of Arminius in one slim paragraph. Part of the reason for our lack of knowledge about Arminius is the dearth of printed material by him or about him. He did not write the volumes that Luther and Calvin did. Dr. Carl Bangs followed his 1958 Ph.D. thesis on "Arminius and Reformed Theology" at the University of Chicago with a biography and a career of writing and speaking about him. But this scholarship is recent.

But regardless of the limited print on Arminius, his contribution to the Reformation movement was truly great. He tried to liberalize the severe Dutch Calvinist views on predestination but to little avail. The state church triumphed over him politically, and it was left to the forerunners of the next century to move on his idea of man's free will as the doorway to God's grace. His greatest influence was on the theology of John Wesley and the Methodists. There was really no reason for the altar call unless man has the responsibility of choice. Modern citywide crusade evangelism stands on Calvinism but practices free will when it comes time for the invitation.

After the death of Arminius, his followers joined in writing a creedal statement called "The Remonstrance," presented in The Hague and signed by 42 ministers and 2 educators. The year was 1610, just 100 years before the decade in which Jonathan Edwards and John and Charles Wesley were born. The Remonstrance contained five articles that were considered the irreducible minimum of Arminian theology.

1. Conditional predestination. Arminius believed that

God determined before the foundation of the world to save, through Christ, whoever believed on Him and did persevere in their faith and obedience to Him.

2. Universality of the Atonement. Jesus Christ died for all men and for every man. However, no man enjoys this forgiveness without becoming a believer. No race, color, or culture is excluded from the doorway to salvation.

3. The new birth is essential. Since man has no saving grace of his own, he must be born again of God through the Holy Spirit.

4. Grace can be resisted. The Scriptures speak of many who resisted the Holy Spirit. Luke reports on the philosophers of Mars' Hill, the silversmiths in Ephesus, King Agrippa, and many others whose resistance to the Holy Spirit is in the narrative of Acts.

5. Conditional perseverance. Those who are in Christ have full power to strive against Satan, sin, the world, and their own flesh. Perseverance comes through the assisting grace of the Holy Spirit.

Although James Arminius is a less-familiar name than Luther and Calvin, he is still a great landmark on the road back to New Testament gospel, our lost estate.

* * *

However, the Protestant Reformation of itself did not return the church full circle to the proclamation of the plain, simple, New Testament gospel with its emphasis on personal salvation. The Lutherans became the state church in Germany. The Calvinists became the state church in Switzerland, Holland, and Scotland, and greatly influenced the government and worship of the Puritans in New England. And state churches usually come down on the side of political authority, birthright membership, and creeds, not on the side of warmhearted Christian experience. There was at least one more step in focusing evangelical fervor on personal salvation by choice. This step was made by the Pietists. And the same encyclopedia that gives minor attention to James Arminius omits the Pietists altogether. But that does not negate their influence. If their influence was silent, it was nonetheless powerful.

Years ago when Billy Graham was holding his first campaign in the Cow Palace in San Francisco, I was a student in Berkeley at Pacific School of Religion. One morning during the campaign Billy Graham came to speak to a gathering of students from all five of the seminaries in the Bay area.

In the next class following the address by Dr. Graham, the professor asked us what we thought about him. I was about the third one to speak when I suggested it seemed good to hear a preacher say without any equivocation or embarrassment, "My Bible says . . ."

The professor was leaning against the wall on the opposite side of the room. But when I came down on the side of Billy's confidence in the Bible, he fairly flew across the room and, standing before my front row seat, shook his finger in my face and said, "Young man, are you trying to separate scholarship from evangelism?"

I sat there speechless and thoroughly intimidated until a Texas student with a slow drawl actually stood to his feet and stopped the teacher dead in his tracks. "I'll tell you one thing, Professor: Billy packs out the Cow Palace and turns away thousands when you liberals could not get 200 people to come and listen to you talk about your doubts." He sat down in the midst of silence that, some seconds later, exploded with applause.

This tension between scholarship and evangelism is probably a standoff that goes back, at least, to Paul's sermon to the philosophers on Mars' Hill. I guess it is too bad that, to borrow a phrase from James Denney, our theologians are not evangelists and our evangelists are not theologians.

Pietism was to the Lutheran church what Methodism was to the Church of England. In the centuries following Luther, the Protestant church in Germany had given itself to scholarly dogmatism, which was seen primarily in the writing of carefully worded statements that accurately described what Luther had taught.

The Pietists, however, were interested in changing the focus of the church from scholastics to experience. They wanted to revive the existing church by the infusion of new life in the Spirit. They wanted to separate the theology of the heart from the cold statements of intellectual orthodoxy. They were more concerned about ethical living than they were with dogmatic beliefs that could be attested and debated to the exclusion of heartfelt experience. They recognized a subjective factor in religion that was more important to them than creedal statements. They were seeking the vital experience of New Testament Christians. They found this simplicity of heart in three ideas that centered in personal, spiritual experience.

1. The new birth as a sudden transformation. A mental acceptance of a theological statement was not enough for the Pietists. As Dr. Taylor writes, "They insisted that a miracle could take place in the will and emotions of a person that would lift his life to a permanently higher level." On the negative side, this transformation required repentance that was demonstrated in turning away from sin, and a denial of the world and its pleasures. On the positive side, this transformation demanded a faith that resulted in salvation and a new life.

2. Witness of the Spirit. The authority of the scriptural promises were attested in the inner testimony of the Spirit. The witness of the Spirit was the privilege of each believer.

3. Regeneration is followed by sanctification. Believing for salvation is always followed by a personal quest for holiness. Sanctification raises the life of a believer to a level above willful transgression of God's law. Sanctification in the believer brings a separation from worldliness. For this reason the Pietists had unreserved condemnation of the theater, all theatrical plays, the dance, and any other expressions of worldliness as they saw them.

Like the Pietists who wanted to return to the simple life of the early Christians, the Moravian church, under the leadership of Count von Zinzendorf, not only believed in personal salvation by faith through Jesus Christ but also felt impelled to do missionary work with great vigor. The first Moravian missionaries came to America in 1735. And in God's providence, they were sailing on the same little vessel that brought John and Charles Wesley to Georgia. Largely through their witness on the ship and by other Moravians back in London, John and Charles Wesley were converted and began immediately to seek holiness. Through the Moravians, another major step was made toward a return to New Testament gospel.

Luther, Calvin, and Arminius were the great Reformation influences who brought the church along the pathway back to New Testament persuasion. And the Pietists, and their stepchild the Moravians, were a less-known but important influence with the forerunners of the altar service. These forerunners—Wesley, Edwards, and Whitefield—will be examined in the next chapter.

6 ☰

Forerunners of the Public Invitation

THREE MEN, more than any others, became the fore-runners of the public invitation and the altar service. Two of these men, John Wesley and Jonathan Edwards, were born the same year, 1703. Wesley led an 18th-century revival in England that historians say changed British history and saved England from a bloody revolution that was experienced by their near neighbor, France, just over 20 miles across the English Channel.

The second forerunner was Jonathan Edwards, a principal in the 18th-century revival in America that gained a heading in history books under The Great Awakening. He is the American who personalized Calvinism and thereby opened the way for the great succession of evangelists and pastors who have fed revival fires in America for nearly 250 years.

The third forerunner of the public invitation was George Whitefield, an Englishman, 11 years younger than John Wesley and Jonathan Edwards, a contemporary who enthralled great throngs of people in open-air meetings in both England and America. It may be said that he was the first professional evangelist (he never held a settled pastorate), who opened up the way for the long line of evangelists who have followed in his wake.

According to an unpublished Ph.D. dissertation by William Oscar Thompson, none of these three men ever gave a public invitation. However, they preached personal salvation and urged people toward a heartfelt experience in Christ.

Mr. Wesley

John Wesley's life spanned most of the 18th century. He was born in a parsonage of the Church of England at Epworth in 1703 and died in his London house adjacent to his Methodist chapel in 1791. During the intervening years Wesley traveled 250,000 miles on horseback in England, Ireland, and Scotland. He wrote, edited, or published more than 400 books and tracts and worked with his brother Charles, who wrote 6,000 hymns. When Wesley died, there were 175,000 people enrolled in his Methodist classes for spiritual growth and development, led by 630 lay preachers.

Several major factors contributed to the great productivity of John and his younger brother Charles: (1) Their mother, Susanna, was an indomitable woman who taught her children at home and presided over the growth and development of their lives. (2) At five years of age John was the last child in his family to be saved from the Epworth parsonage just before its fiery collapse. He was highly motivated for all his adult years as "a brand plucked from the burning." Since his life had been saved, there must have been a reason. (3) He had a quality education in Charterhouse School in London and at Oxford University. (4) After years of trying to gain his salvation by his disciplined life, he was warmly converted during a Moravian meeting in London. (5) Holiness became a lifelong passion. (6) He had the flexibility and organizational genius that resulted in the small-group idea for his converts. And, (7) he used laymen as spiritual leaders.

On the North Atlantic crossing of the boat carrying John and his brother, Charles, to Georgia, they experienced a severe storm that made them despair for their lives. But in the midst of their devastating fear, they observed that the Moravian missionary families on board showed no fear at all. Even their children laughed and sang during the worst of the storm. When John and Charles inquired about the unconcern of the Moravians, the Germans were quick to tell them about the assurance of their personal salvation.

After 28 frustrating months (only 10 months for Charles) John was back in London, feeling he had failed to convert the Indians as well as himself. Once again, John crossed paths with a Moravian who would not give up on him. Eventually the last barrier was broken down, and John, in attendance at a Moravian meeting in Aldersgate Street, experienced personal salvation. His "heart was strangely warmed." Almost immediately John left London on a 3-month trip to the headquarters of the Moravians in Germany, but not before he made a significant entry into his daily *Journal:*

"In the evening I went very unwillingly to a society in Aldersgate Street . . . About a quarter before nine . . . I felt I did trust in Christ, Christ alone for my salvation; and an assurance was given me that He had taken away *my* sins, even *mine*, and saved *me*, from the law of sin and death."

When John returned to London in the early fall of 1738, it seemed the people of the British Isles were primed for some kind of spiritual awakening. Other European countries had their spiritual heroes. Luther had been the recognized leader in Germany. Calvin was the giant among religious leaders in Switzerland. John Knox returned to Scotland from his exile in Geneva to stir the Scots in a new spiritual awakening. James Arminius may not have been the religious hero of the Netherlands, but the Dutch were very much aware of the controversy his message had generated. However, England had never felt the exhilaration that comes from a national infection of new religious vitality. England needed a revival. And, although they did not know it, they were ready, like a tinder box, to explode into religious flame.

*　　*　　*

The background of England's need for revival began with Henry VIII. During the early 1500s, King Henry VIII had cut the lines that tied England to Rome but failed to lift the spiritual level of England when Parliament, by his urging, made the king himself the official head of the church. When Mary, Henry's daughter by the first of his six wives, became queen of England, she determined to return the church to the Catholic fold. She became known as Bloody Mary for her merciless persecutions. More than 300 persons, including the most high-ranking Protestants, were burned at her stakes.

After the five-year reign of terror under Queen Mary I, Elizabeth I came to the throne, giving the government and the people promise of almost a half century—1558 to 1603—of stability. She assured the people that the Church of England would be reinstated as Protestant. With this word the exiles began returning from the Continent. But with them, they brought some new religious ideas they had learned in places like the Netherlands, Germany, and Geneva. The Calvinists were critical of the established church and wanted to purify its ways. This surge of Puritanism was an irritant of increasing frustration to church leaders. When the *Mayflower* sailed off to the New World in 1620, a significant contingency of the people called Puritans was on board, ready to transport their religious ideas to the New World.

Unfortunately the Puritans who remained in England centered their agitation primarily on the organization of the church and not on matters relating to personal salvation. Religion fell into disfavor in the British Isles. The churches were mostly empty. Morals disintegrated. And religion was not even a fit subject for educated people to discuss. It was out-of-date. Rectorships were political appointments to be bought or given as favors for loyalty. Even John Wesley's mother and father suffered a difficult estrangement because of Samuel's loyalty to the crown, which after all was the source of his appointment. Susanna persisted in her harsh criticism of the king's policies until a serious breach occurred in their relationship.

This state of spiritual lethargy and religious disarray conditioned the soil and made England ripe for the spiritual awakening John and Charles Wesley were to lead. Several salient characteristics identify the spiritual genius of the Wesley brothers as forerunners of the public invitation and the altar service. Although they did not use a public altar in their outdoor services, the spirit of the altar and the altar call was even with them.

1. Wesley communicated to the common people where they were. Luther gave the people the Bible in the vernacular. John Wesley gave the people his message on the people's terms, preaching in the out-of-doors, at the entrances to mines, in city parks, even from the tombstone of his father in the churchyard of Epworth. He left his manuscripts at home and preached extemporaneously. He prided himself in using short, understandable words. He communicated with music that taught New Testament doctrine. And he preached for a verdict.

When Wesley first considered George Whitefield's challenge to preach in the open air, he said, "I should have thought the saving of souls almost a sin if it had not been done in a church." But field preaching was more than outdoor services. It was meeting the people where they were. In the fields there was no Sunday morning dress code, no imposing doors to pull open, no strange faces to search for signs of social acceptance. Because Wesley was willing to take his message where the people were, he preached to crowds of up to 20,000, while in the churches he would have had a few hundred at most.

2. Wesley was the first preacher since the time of the apostles to unleash the spiritual energies of laymen in ministry. By deputizing a cohort of laymen under his leadership, Wesley multiplied his own energies hundreds of times over. These men were not ordained, but they could exhort sinners and deliver their messages. As a result thousands were converted. Furthermore, they led hundreds of classes of new believers in the spiritual disciplines of a holy life.

John Wesley resisted the idea of lay preaching. Laymen were not ordained, and most of them had never attended Oxford or Cambridge. This time it was not George Whitefield who changed Wesley's mind but his mother, Susanna. John was upset because Thomas Maxwell, an exhorter, had gone beyond his bounds by expounding the Scriptures. Susanna came to the rescue of the lay preacher by standing up to her strong-willed son in the way a strong-willed mother could speak: "John . . . take care what you do with respect to that young man, for he is as surely called of God to preach as you are. Examine . . . the fruits of his preaching, and hear him for yourself." John responded with an uncharacteristic flexibility. He heard the layman speak and concluded, "It is the Lord. Let Him do what seemeth good."

With Wesley's dramatic move to use lay ministers, he began a program of education designed to accompany their level of grace. He was not going to allow sanctified ignorance. He required five hours of study per day. He wrote books for them. He prepared lists of books for them, covering a wide range of subjects from astronomy to Old Testament Hebrew. He often taught them personally. A special library, divided into 12 sections of books, was kept available to these lay preachers in three places they were likely to frequent— Bristol, Newcastle, and London. It is not surprising that he not only defended his lay preachers against the charge of ignorance but also once compared them favorably with the students he himself had taught at Oxford. This daring move to use lay preachers made it possible for Asbury to develop the great concept of the circuit-riding preachers on the American frontier.

3. The Wesley brothers introduced the idea of the evangelistic hymn. Luther wrote hymns, as did Isaac Watts, such as "Alas, and Did My Savior Bleed?" But no one before them used music in the propagation of revival like John and Charles Wesley. Charles wrote a hymn on the night of his conversion and celebrated the occasion with a series of anniversary hymns. Their music, like their preaching, commu-

nicated the gospel at a level the people could grasp. They were severely criticized for "Jesus, Lover of My Soul" because of its emotional overtones. When John was in London, Charles rode over to his house on horseback each day, usually composing a hymn as he rode. Anticipating a new hymn, the servant met Charles to take his horse and to give him a pen and paper for writing down his new hymn. Hundreds of their hymns lived. But all of them were written for one purpose only: to bring men to God through Jesus Christ.

Pastor Jonathan Edwards

In the year 1703 two proud mothers had sons destined for greatness in church history. Although one son was born in England and the other in America, the mothers chose very similar names. The Wesley baby born in Epworth was named John. And the Edwards baby born in East Windsor, Conn., was named Jonathan.

John Wesley came out of an Anglican high church background with its emphasis on the authority of the church through the sacraments. But he proclaimed the gospel of free will, which he learned from the Arminians, and the experience of personal salvation by faith through Jesus Christ, which he learned from the Moravians, confirmed by the Scriptures and his own personal experience.

Jonathan Edwards came from the Congregational background of New England Calvinism with its emphasis on predestination and the church of the elect. When the families of second- and third-generation church members did not meet the standards of the church by showing evidences of election, the idea of the Halfway Covenant was born. The Halfway Covenant allowed parents to have their children baptized but kept them from full membership in the church and from receiving Communion. By 1735 full church membership was restricted to a small minority in New England. The Halfway Covenant had salvaged the church by making it possible for families who did not call themselves Christian to be included in its fellowship. But the dilution of spiritual vitality through the Halfway Convenant was disastrous. It was this Halfway Covenant and what it had done toward un-Christianizing New England that troubled Jonathan Edwards.

Edwards, like Wesley, had the right credentials. He came from a family that had provided many Congregational pastors. He was a Yale graduate, entering the university at age 13. At age 23 he became assistant pastor of the Congregational Church in Northampton, Mass. Two years later, on the death of the Northampton pastor, who was his grandfather, Jonathan Edwards took over full responsibility of the church, which he held until 1750. Worn out early, he died at 55 years of age.

With 90 percent of the population outside the church, what New England needed was not a better accommodation with the halfway people but a revival. In 1734 Jonathan Edwards began a series of messages on justification by faith in which he swept away the sacramental theology of the people. And, as William Warren Sweet says in *Revivalism in America,* he "personalized Calvinism."

1. Jonathan Edwards tilted Calvinistic theology toward human responsibility. He maintained two pillars of faith, the sovereignty of God and the sinfulness of man. There is no doubt Edwards believed he had not compromised Calvin's theology; but intended or unintended, the personalization of Calvinism was under way. The floodgate was cracked open for the unending flow of evangelism that issued from reformed theology. But it was evangelism in the tradition of Calvin adjusted for personal responsibility.

2. Jonathan Edwards, along with John Wesley, legitimized emotion in religious experience. People who groaned or cried out, "What must I do to be saved?" were not ejected from their meetings. Jonathan Edwards admonished them to be saved. He organized times of singing outside the regular services, where highly charged emotions could spend themselves in an orderly fashion. He did not let services get out of

hand, but he gave emotion in church a new legitimacy that fit the developing mold of evangelism.

3. Jonathan Edwards developed methods for dealing with converts. Although he did not have class meetings as John Wesley did, Edwards encouraged seekers to meet in groups in their homes to pray and help each other. He brought some specific groups together—young people, children, older people—and instructed them himself in the ways of salvation. Those who were the most deeply convicted were invited to the parsonage for spiritual counseling. The most popular place of meeting in Northampton shifted from the tavern to the pastor's home. There is no indication Jonathan Edwards ever gave an invitation for seekers to come forward for prayer, but he did open the door for the future development of the public invitation.

As a forerunner of the public invitation, Edwards was blessed with unusual evangelistic success. In a town of 1,100 people, 300 were converted, and 100 joined the church within a six-month period. The spread of this revival across New England and its extension along the Eastern seaboard through the preaching of George Whitefield has long since made the history books as The Great Awakening.

George Whitefield

A third forerunner of the public invitation and the altar service was George Whitefield. He was born in an English inn at Gloucester on December 14, 1714. His background was totally different from that of the Wesley brothers and Jonathan Edwards. He was raised in a subculture far removed from parsonage life as it was known in either Epworth or New England. He was exposed to the spiritually debilitating atmosphere that characterized the English pub in those days, when a man could get drunk for a penny and dead drunk for two cents. Clean straw for sleeping off a hangover was free.

Although he was younger than either of the Wesleys,

Whitefield went to Oxford, where he met them through the Holy Club. Like the other club members who subjected themselves to the strictest kinds of religious discipline and to works of Christian service, George Whitefield became spiritually frustrated. After a year of seeking, including two months of intense spiritual groaning, George Whitefield was suddenly set free. Having cast himself on Christ, he was genuinely converted.

A year after his conversion Whitefield was ordained to preach, and within another year he was a national phenomenon. Huge crowds, which the churches could never contain, thronged to hear George Whitefield preach. Troublesome to the established church, but loved by the throngs who came to hear him, Whitefield turned to the open fields, where his sermons were heard by even bigger crowds.

As a forerunner of the public invitation, Whitefield had the unique role of professional evangelist on both sides of the Atlantic. In fact, he crossed the ocean in a boat 13 times. Both the Wesley brothers and Jonathan Edwards were his admirers. Benjamin Franklin was greatly impressed by his preaching. The actor Garrick said that Whitefield could make people cry by the way he said, "Mesopotamia." The two poets William Cowper and John Greenleaf Whittier extolled his virtues. Even the infidel philosopher David Hume (1711-76) said he would go 20 miles to hear him preach.

There is no record that Whitefield ever gave a public invitation. However, there were many days when he was kept busy with spiritual counseling from early morning until well into the night by seekers who came to him following his sermons. His successes in Bath, Bristol, and London just before he sailed for America in 1739 were phenomenal. Aside from his ample natural gifts, how did George Whitefield contribute to evangelism as a forerunner of the public invitation?

1. Whitefield brought all denominations to hear the gospel as well as great throngs of unbelievers. He bridged denominational barriers. He preached to 15,000 in the Boston Common, a cross section of the population. He was a

forerunner of citywide campaigns because of the unity he brought to evangelism in many cities where he preached.

2. Whitefield was a Calvinist who preached like an Arminian. This adjustment of Calvinism toward personal responsibility and free will in evangelism caused H. Orton Wiley to write: "Arminianism is the only successful doctrinal system . . . In all cases of revival in the church where success attends, Calvinists are compelled to surrender for the time being their Calvinistic doctrines of predestination and reprobation, and preach and teach Arminianism, or the provision of salvation for all men."

Whitefield spread the "new birth" theology and message through all the colonies. He had the capacity to visualize concepts like justification by faith, which made it possible for him to preach in graphic pictures.

George Whitefield was the model for a new kind of preaching that deserted manuscripts for word pictures delivered extemporaneously. In fact, written copies of Whitefield's sermons do not read well, since they were prepared for oral delivery.

3. George Whitefield gave life to the idea of full-time professional evangelists who preached for decisions and called for a regenerate church. For 250 years the fortunes of professional, full-time evangelists have, like the stock market, risen and fallen in successive waves. But through good times and bad, the cadre of evangelists in evangelical churches can trace their heritage back to George Whitefield.

Unfortunately, George Whitefield failed at the point of nurturing converts. However, his lack of follow-through on new Christians highlighted this need for other pastors and evangelists who were to follow him. Although Whitefield was in some ways a greater evangelist than John Wesley, his work was less enduring. Whitefield said, "My brother Wesley acted more wisely than I. The souls that were awakened in his ministry, he joined together in classes, and so preserved the fruit of his labors. I failed to do this, and as a result, my people are a rope of sand."

In the growth and development of the public invitation and the altar service, Jonathan Edwards' personalized Calvinism seemed to lead the way toward the method that called people forward to an inquiry room or prayer room for spiritual counseling. John Wesley's Arminian emphasis on free will and personal responsibility tended to lead the way toward an open altar where seekers gather in the company of friends and spiritual leaders who pray for them to receive a personal experience of salvation, which leads them on to holiness and entire sanctification. Whitefield led the way in citywide campaigns and the interdenominational approach in preaching for a decision.

The pathfinders: Luther, Calvin, Arminius, and the Pietists helped the church find its way back to personal salvation by faith proclaimed in New Testament persuasion. These pathfinders were followed by the forerunners of the public invitation and the altar service, Wesley, Edwards, and Whitefield. And now we turn to the evangelistic trailblazers on the American frontier who cleared new ground in camp meetings, circuit riding, church revivals, citywide campaigns, and finally, the altar in evangelistic churches. These men in succession are Bishop Francis Asbury, Evangelist Charles G. Finney, and Pastor-evangelist Phineas F. Bresee.

DIVISION THREE

The Altar Comes of Age

Time is now fleeting; the moments are passing,
Passing from you and from me.
Shadows are gathering; death's night is coming,
Coming for you and for me.
—from the hymn "Softly and Tenderly"

7

Francis Asbury and the Methodist Mourner's Bench

O N THE WALL in the President's Conference Room at Olivet Nazarene University is a copy of the painting by Kenneth Wyatt of John Wesley saying good-bye to Coke and Asbury, who were ready to sail to America as his representatives. Wesley's instructions were contained in three words: "Give them Christ."

This print, which was distributed by the United Methodist church during the celebration of its 200th anniversary in America, puts the mind to wondering: Wesley said, "Give them Christ," but he did not prescribe the methods by which the Savior was to be given to a wild and vigorous new country. This left Asbury open to innovation. Field preaching in England was replaced with the camp meeting in America. The itinerant ministry made way for the circuit-riding preachers on the frontier, and Methodist chapels became Methodist Episcopal churches. But there was one new idea that was no transplant from England. It was America's own idea: the Methodist mourner's bench.

Wesley's spiritual children in America received Christ through a new church that took the place of the Methodist chapels in England. They received Christ through an ordained itinerant clergy who rode horseback into every nook and cranny of the frontier. They received Christ through a new kind of music that expressed the hopes and fears of the believers, even their ecstasy. They received Christ through the camp meetings, which got mixed reviews, along with the Methodist revivals, which were an adaptation of the camp meeting brought to town. But most of all they received Christ through heartwarming preaching that focused on a spiritual decision. And ultimately this decision for Christ was directly related to an experience at a mourner's bench or altar.

Jesse Lee and other first-generation American Methodists connected the idea of the public invitation to Bishop Francis Asbury. Dr. Robert Coleman, in *The Origin of the Altar Call in American Methodism,* says, "What might have been the first public invitation of this type was given at a little Methodist church in Maryland in 1798." This was less than 15 years after the founding of the Methodist church at the Christmas Conference in Baltimore in 1784.

In his journal Jesse Lee says Mr. Asbury preached on Eph. 5:25-27. In the King James Version, this passage reads as follows:

> Husbands, love your wives,
> even as Christ also loved the church,
> and gave himself for it;
> that he might sanctify and cleanse it
> with the washing of water by the word,
> that he might present it to himself a glorious church,
> not having spot, or wrinkle, or any such thing;
> but that it should be holy and without blemish.

After the sermon, Rev. Jesse Lee exhorted the people as "many wept, and some cried aloud with deep distress." Following a second exhortation by a Miles Harper, the congregation was dismissed while those interested in spiritual things were asked to stay. A third man, John Easter, "began to sing, and in a little while many were afflicted, and a general weeping began." Bishop Asbury requested that all who were under conviction come together.

Jesse Lee concludes the entry in his journal by saying, "Several men and women came and fell upon their knees; and the preachers, for some time, kept singing, and exhorting the mourners to expect a blessing from the Lord. . . . Then prayer was made in behalf of the mourners, and two or three found peace." Coleman says this practice of calling convicted people to a designated place marks the actual beginning of the altar call as a part of the Methodist service.

The mourner's bench, a crude, backless bench placed forward for the convenience of the seekers, became an important new piece of church furniture. The mourner's bench was the natural result of an appeal at the end of the sermon for sinners to be saved and for believers to be sanctified. Sinners and believers knelt at the mourner's bench for special encounters with God.

Within a quadrennium of the first altar call recorded in Jesse Lee's *Diary*, the idea caught hold. In June of 1800 Francis Asbury received a letter from one of his preachers that read, "On the Sabbath after you left here, about one hundred and nine came forward." In May of 1801 a preacher from Connecticut reported to Asbury on an open-air service where 83 came forward. In April of 1802 at a crowded meetinghouse, "A great number of mourners came to us in prayer when the invitation was given." Dr. Coleman concludes his references to the early records of public invitations with a quote from the journal of circuit rider Henry Smith, dated Sunday, May 29, 1803: "I then proposed for those who were mourning to know the love of God, if they would come forward and kneel down. Eight or ten came."

Dr. Coleman rejects the assertion of some historians who suggest that the mourner's bench was put to first use in the winter of 1807 in a New York City chapel. The same rejection holds good for the idea of the mourner's bench as a product of the backwoods camp meetings, or even the suggestion that this procedure was one of Charles G. Finney's new measures.

There is no doubt that some pastors with established

churches, complete with Communion rails where communicants were invited forward to receive the Lord's Supper, had but one small step to make in the new evangelism procedure of asking seekers to come forward and kneel at the rail. In fact, the first camp meetings in Kentucky grew out of meetings planned primarily for serving the Lord's Supper to the frontiersmen who had no church to attend regularly and no ordained ministers to serve them Communion. Because these meetings drew large crowds, the services were moved from the church to the out-of-doors.

It was this association of the altar and the coming forward of the people for Communion that gave birth to the "altar call." In most churches, a rail was built to separate the people from the sacred altar, or the sacred table on which the Communion elements were placed. This rail was a natural focus for coming to Christ or seeking a spiritual experience. No historian has claimed that the public invitation, as an evangelistic technique, was invented by Francis Asbury; but no discussion of the Methodist mourner's bench and the accompanying altar call can be separated from the pervasive influence of this evangelist made bishop. Francis Asbury traveled the American frontier for more than 40 years in response to John Wesley's admonition at the harbor in Bristol, "Give them Christ."

Francis Asbury Time Line

1745

Francis Asbury was born on August 20, 1745, in Staffordshire, England. His birthplace was north of Birmingham, a city of the industrial revolution. John Wesley was already hard at work in leading this spiritual revolution that would change England. America was still 31 years short of its Declaration of Independence.

1760-66

Francis Asbury was converted at 15 years of age. About a year later he had a great spiritual experience. Some called it sanctification. By age 17 he was exhorting and preaching in public meetings. At age 21 he received his first appointment as a traveling Methodist preacher. Francis Asbury had found his destiny.

1771

During a conference in Bristol Mr. Wesley called for volunteers to go to America. Three weeks later Asbury was on the deck of a sailing vessel in Bristol harbor, outfitted with a new change of clothes. His friends raised money for him to own two blankets and to rent a sleeping space on the deck, but not the luxury of a protected place below. With constant exposure and fatigue, it is no wonder he suffered from chronic seasickness. He said, "No sickness I ever knew was equal to it." After 53 days on the North Atlantic, Francis Asbury landed at Philadelphia on October 27, 1771. He was 26 years old.

1775-83

As an Englishman committed to John Wesley, Asbury curtailed his work during the American Revolution, living for a while in Canada. One year before the Declaration of Independence, John Wesley read Samuel Johnson's tract *Taxation No Tyranny* and switched from support of the colonists to support of the king. Wesley's version of Samuel Johnson's tract was published and sold 40,000 copies in a few days. The Tories on both sides of the Atlantic were delighted, and the Patriots were infuriated. Asbury wrote, "I am sorry the venerable man ever dipped into the politics of America."

1784

John Wesley, the lifelong son of the Church of England, finally ordained two men in Bristol, thus opening the way for the ordination of Methodist preachers in America. Thomas Coke, one of the two men ordained by Wesley, sailed with two comrades from Bristol to America in the fall of 1784 with important documents from Wesley. One of these documents was the appointment of Francis Asbury as general superintendent. During the Christmas Conference in Baltimore, when the Methodist church was officially organized in the United States, Francis Asbury was ordained on December 26 and confirmed as general superintendent the following day. In his biography of Asbury, L. C. Rudolph says that Wesley intended to ordain a bishop and call him a superintendent. Asbury's first day's ride as general superintendent was 50 miles through a snowstorm.

1787

The title "Bishop" was used for the first time in the general minutes. Asbury did not accept the idea that bishops and preachers were equal. He believed bishops were chosen to rule.

1809

In the year Abraham Lincoln was born on the Kentucky frontier, Asbury's Methodist evangelism was riding high. His circuit riders and presiding elders got his latest directive: Asbury wanted to see 600 Methodist camp meetings in 1810.

1813-16

Asbury was worn-out and facing death. At the Conference in 1813 he delivered his last message to the presiding elders. During 1814 he kept going by doggedness and his belligerent unwillingness to stop, even when he had to be set on his horse and had to preach sitting down. On December 7, 1815, Bishop Francis Asbury wrote the last entry into his journal. He died on March 31, 1816, at 70 years of age.

Asbury's Theology of Evangelism

Francis Asbury was an unusual man by every standard. John Wesley traveled two small islands with a flat terrain that made it possible for him to read on horseback. Asbury traveled a mountainous territory that soon equaled the size of Europe. Wesley rode from town to town, while Asbury rode from wilderness to wilderness. He crossed the Alleghenies 58 times. In his journal Asbury describes these ascents and descents as the dirtiest trick nature could ever play on a horseman because of the slippery slides in winter and spring. He crawled up the worst places on his hands and knees. And, when there were no ferryboats, he and his horses swam the rivers. In the south he led his horse through swamps. Ordinarily, Asbury rode one horse and used a second for all his earthly belongings. Friends said his packhorse would follow him anywhere and everywhere. He slept in the woods. And a night in a cabin filled with children, critters, and crawling things was not necessarily an improvement on the woods.

Asbury was an early riser, always before 5 A.M.; otherwise he claimed no privacy for prayer and study. He was self-taught, reading the Bible in Greek, Hebrew, and Latin, as well as English. However, prayer was his major concern. He believed the devil would let any preacher read as long as he didn't pray. He saw the sophisticated pastors in the large city churches as men who read widely but did not know any more about saving souls than about catching whales.

Asbury's commitment to the common man is seen in the charge he gave his preachers about the construction of buildings: "Let all our chapels be built plain and decent; but not more expensive than is absolutely necessary. Otherwise the necessity of raising money will make rich men necessary to us. And if so, we must be dependent on them, yea, and governed by them. And then farewell to the Methodist discipline, if not doctrine too."

Bishop Asbury's theology of evangelism reflected John Wesley's idea of the "House of Salvation." The sinner under conviction and guilt stands on the front porch of salvation's house, facing the door. Because of his depravity, the convicted person finds it difficult to take the step of faith across the threshold into the actual "House of Salvation." However, when the step is taken and conversion is attained, the threshold is no place for a new Christian to stop and put down his roots. You can't live long in the doorway. And it's awkward to set up spiritual housekeeping just inside the door. The idea is to occupy the whole house. There comes a moment in spiritual growth and development when the Christian fully possesses his house, and the house fully possesses him. Living in the "House of Salvation" is not a static experience. The goal of evangelism is to help seekers enter the "House of Salvation" and then to make the house their own by cleansing and love. A clean house with clean occupants who are dominated by the emotions and attitudes of love make for a great living experience. People on the frontier could appreciate the need for shelter, even if it were only a cabin, and the twin need of trustworthy relationships. They understood the need for cleanliness and love, whether or not they ever achieved this ideal.

Asbury believed repentance and faith for conversion were man's responsibility. God provided salvation through the death and resurrection of Jesus. God provided the means for entering the threshold of conversion through prevenient grace that enabled all people to repent and believe. Because men were depraved, Asbury believed they needed special direction and encouragement to enter the door by faith.

Asbury believed his preachers should be evangelistic in every sermon. He charged them (1) to convince sinners of their lost condition, (2) to show the awful character of sin by describing its conduct in striking colors, (3) to identify with the sinner by naming and disarming all his excuses against stepping forward to repent and believe, and finally, (4) to stay with the sinner, seeing him across the threshold with prayer and admonition.

Since the crossing was often tumultuous and usually associated with the idea of human struggle, the moment of conversion came with the great sense of relief and joy often expressed in shouts of victory. Shouting Methodists, who might be motivated to shout again at reminders of their crossing, became a religious phenomenon on the frontier. Shouting was a means of assurance. The crossing had really been made.

The Baptists and the Methodists were not far apart in their ideas of conversion. They both focused clearly on the threshold of the "House of Salvation." But sanctification was another matter. Both Baptists and Methodists believed in sanctification, but Baptists saw sanctification as a long, uphill journey toward spiritual maturity to be perfected only at death. Asbury, like Wesley, believed that Christians would grow as long as they lived. They saw sanctification as an instantaneous experience, both preceded and followed by growth. Christian perfection was attainable in this life and was to be lifted up to believing Christians as an experience to be sought.

Asbury relied on John Wesley's *Plain Account of Christian Perfection* as the standard in his own theology of evangelism. The following passage from that classic account is central in understanding what Asbury believed about Christian perfectionism or entire sanctification.

1. By perfection I mean the humble, gentle, patient love of God and our neighbor, ruling our tempers, words, and actions.

I do not include an impossibility of falling from it, either in part or in whole. Therefore, I retract several expressions in our hymns, which partly express, partly imply, such an impossibility.

And I do not contend for the term sinless, though I do not object against it.

2. As to the manner, I believe this perfection is always wrought in the soul by a simple act of faith; consequently in an instant. But I believe in a gradual work both preceding and following that instant.

3. As to time, I believe this instant generally is the instant of death, the moment before the soul leaves the body. But I believe it may be ten, twenty, or forty years before.

Asbury preached sanctification and Christian perfection because he believed it. But he also had another motivation. His converts by the thousands came out of nonchurched areas where there was little spiritual background and religious atmosphere to help keep them spiritually connected. He could preach against backsliding, and he did. But it seemed to Asbury and his Methodist preachers that the real answer to drifting faith and diluted morals was to lead believers into the experience of heart holiness. As he grew older and Methodist evangelism became more structured, Asbury felt an even greater urge to preach holiness. He believed in preaching holiness in every sermon. Quarterly meeting statistics during this era included not only the number of new church members but also the number of persons converted and the number sanctified. Methodist evangelism had hit its full stride.

John Peters, in *Christian Perfection in American Methodism,* makes a point of the changes in transplanting the theology of sanctification from England to America. However, the changes were more in process than content. Since Asbury's purpose was to replace a Christian's "first love" with "pure love," he never hesitated to urge new believers on into the experience of heart holiness. The fruit of this evangelism was more visible at the mourner's bench than in the class meeting. People who had been saved at the mourner's bench could naturally look forward to being sanctified at the same place. The death of self was like the death of the person; it might be a long time coming, but there was an instant when it happened. This was the moment for shouting.

Asbury and the Camp Meeting

Charles Johnson, in his book *The American Camp Meeting,* gives credit to a fiery Presbyterian preacher named McGready for the first planned camp meeting in America. Thompson, in his Ph.D. dissertation on the public invitation, confirms the fact. It happened in July of 1800 at the Presbyterian church on the Red River in Kentucky when people came together the first time for the purpose of holding religious services while they camped nearby.

The next year, in 1801, came the famous Cane Ridge Camp Meeting, a few miles east of present-day Lexington, Ky. Attendance was estimated from 10,000 to 25,000. There were no newspaper advertisements, no telephones, no radio.

Just the word of mouth from the Methodists, the circuit riders, and other itinerants who spread the news. But they came in Conestoga wagons, full family contingents, prepared with slabs of bacon, supplies of beef, hams, chickens, and all the other groceries needed for a six-day stay.

Preachers preached when and wherever the Spirit seemed to move. Several preached at once from fallen logs, tree stumps, wagon beds, or raised knolls of grass, all respectfully distant from each other. There were no assigned singers who came to entertain or lead. The favorite hymn was Isaac Watts' "Am I a Soldier of the Cross?" Preachers preached until people fell under the Spirit and the spontaneous prayer meeting was on. In the evening, the flicker of fires, the shadow movements among the wagons, and the singing of the people formed an unforgettable montage of sight and sound. It would have been impossible for the campers not to feel that something great and extraordinary was going on.

Most writers have dramatized these meetings rather than analyzed their meaning in terms of the frontier needs they met. They are easier to depict than to dissect. To say the least, the established city churches in the East were scandalized to hear that men and women were praying together, that people shouted and jerked, and that souls were converted in an instant with no follow-up teaching and established instruction. But for good or ill, the camp meeting could not be ignored. And the prospects for its future were undimmed.

The Presbyterians soon withdrew because they did not have the temperament for the emotional responses of camp meeting. The Baptist frontier preachers did not suffer over the emotional excesses headlined in the papers of the East, but they lacked the organization to take advantage of the camp meeting movement as a powerful evangelistic means. Not so with Asbury and the Methodists. They loved the noise and the emotional intensity. And they had the network through their districts and quarterly meeting structure to take advantage of what they saw as a great evangelism opportunity.

The Methodist church never adopted the camp meeting officially, never passed any denominational laws to control it, and from 1800 through 1845, when its peak had passed, there were few references to camp meetings in conference reports and minutes. The lack of official oversight may have fanned its growth. With oversight usually comes restraint.

However, by 1805 Asbury and his Methodists had taken over evangelism through the camp meeting. Asbury went against the tide of migration by sending the camp meeting east, where the bigger population centers could benefit. In the meantime, he led the Methodists in planning camp meetings within reach of every cabin. After riding the Ohio circuits in the summer of 1809, Asbury reported that every district had its own camp meeting.

The very heart of the camp meeting was the pulpit, the Communion table, and the mourner's bench. The Methodist message was preached from the pulpit, the mourners were invited to the altar, and before the camp was adjourned, they all took part in a great Communion service. Believers were invited to receive the elements of the Lord's Supper. On the final day, they took their places in the double column that marched around the camp, singing a militant hymn, saying good-byes, shaking hands, and reminding themselves that they were going home to serve as Christian soldiers. By 1810 the camp meeting mourner's bench and the altar call had become standard procedure for Methodists, both East and West, in the cities and on the frontier. The altar call and the camp meeting had risen separately but simultaneously.

Bishop Asbury and the Circuit Riders

When Francis Asbury arrived in Baltimore in 1771, five years before the Declaration of Independence was signed, he established the Methodist idea of an itinerant ministry. The way to keep up with a population on the move was to provide preachers on the move.

First of all, Asbury set the example as an itinerant himself. He never owned a house or even rented one. He made no advance arrangements for boarding. He simply bought a horse and started on the long ride that lasted for more than 45 years. Only death would stop him. He never married, because marriage would have been unfair to his wife. She could not travel with him, and his long absences from her would have been intolerable for both of them.

Methodists were organized into classes, or house churches, held together by a circuit rider who visited the groups on a fairly systematic basis. Most circuits took four or six weeks to cover. The circuits were part of a district presided over by an elder, appropriately called presiding elder. Each district held a quarterly conference and an annual conference. The ruling body of the denomination was the General Conference, which met every four years.

When America signed the Treaty of Peace with Great Britain at the close of the Revolutionary War in 1783, the territory of the United States was instantly extended westward to the Mississippi. With generous congressional land offers as the lure, thousands of people began to pour across the mountains into the Ohio River Valley. In 1792 Kentucky was admitted to the Union, and in 1796 Tennessee followed suit. By 1790, only seven years after the end of the war, 120,000 people lived west of the Appalachian Mountains. The circuit riders of the Methodist church were prepared to serve these people.

These preachers on horseback saturated the frontier, leaving the impact of their message everywhere they went. A frustrated Presbyterian said he would like to go up to just one cabin door where a Methodist circuit rider had not already been. The impact of their message was demonstrated by a man in Kentucky who put a poultice around his wife's head in an effort to draw out her Methodist thinking. This indefatigable spirit of the circuit rider gave rise to the expression "No one would be out on a night like this but a Methodist circuit rider."

But the success of the Methodist preachers was the focus

of their method and their message on the mourner's bench and all it stood for. They were unlearned but not ignorant. Asbury, like Wesley, charged them to study five hours a day, and he provided them the example. They all preached without notes. They knew their Bibles. And they knew human nature, particularly human nature on the frontier. They repeated their own stories of conversion and asked members of their congregations to do the same. They were experience-centered and directed all their sermons toward a decision. The circuit-riding preachers were the Methodist mourner's bench on the move. They did not carry it in their saddlebags along with their Bibles, Methodist Discipline, and the hymn-book, but all the mourner's bench stood for was at the heart of their work.

In 1784, when Methodism became an official church in America, there were 14,988 members. By 1840 there were 825,908 members. This growth is best explained in the work of the Methodist circuit riders and the annual camp meeting, where the impact of religious experience at the mourner's bench was primary.

8

Charles G. Finney
and the Anxious Seat

SOON after the end of the Revolutionary War, an ocean of immigrants in successive waves poured into central and western New York, filling an area 100 miles wide and 200 miles long. Most of these people who developed New York's frontier were Yankees from New England, while most of the wagons lumbering through the Cumberland Gap into Kentucky and Tennessee carried people from the Carolinas and Virginia.

Since England's Treaty of Peace with the United States in 1783 expanded America's territory to the Mississippi River, and since Congress was offering land for as little as $1.25 per acre, there were plenty of takers, thousands of new people looking toward the frontier for a new beginning.

When the first settlers arrived in the Finger Lakes area of New York, these crystal-clear waters were ringed with hills, covered with stately forests, mostly unexplored and seen by only a select few. In 1800 the wilderness of central and western New York was populated by less than 65,000 people, with all but 16,000 of them living in the three eastern counties. Within one generation the population exploded to 750,000, not counting those who had already moved on further west to push back newer frontiers in Ohio and Indiana.

Until 1825 the people of central and western New York lived under the severe conditions of frontier life. However, by

1825, when Charles G. Finney began his ministry, conditions had eased somewhat, physical life was less threatened, law and order had been established, and the usual run of frontier rowdies had moved on to new locations between the Susquehanna and the Monongahela rivers and along their successor, the Ohio River. Most people in upstate New York were enjoying a more settled way of life. There was the vigor of growing cities in places like Utica, Rome, and Troy, but the rip-roaring, robust period of frontier life was being replaced by a more dependable scheme of things. Not least among the new developments in upstate New York was the completion of the Erie Canal in 1825.

Many families from New England had a church connection. Their spiritual sensitivities were increased by the ravages of the War of 1812. And many of them believed they could not be Christian without a conversion experience. Since many of these upstate New Yorkers believed conversions came to most people during revival times, revivals were essential. Therefore, the established churches were susceptible to the wave of revival that was soon to cover central and western New York. A real awakening was waiting to happen, and the person God used to lead the way was Charles Grandison Finney.

As a lawyer and later as an evangelist, Charles G. Finney had a commanding presence. He was 6 feet 2 inches tall, and most people thought he looked even taller. He held himself erect. His facial expressions and body gestures indicated great alertness to everything around him. He was full of energy. People said he walked with an elastic step. Folks on the street instinctively turned to follow him with their eyes.

Finney weighed 185 pounds and was "without an ounce of superfluous flesh." He was physically strong. He loved hunting and was devoted to this sport as long as he could carry a gun. Walking through the woods with a gun cradled across his arm was one of his chief lifetime diversions.

Finney was described generally as a handsome man. But it was his eyes that set him apart from others. One man said that he seemed to read "your inmost thoughts." One of his students at Oberlin later said, "He looked through me until I felt it." However, Finney must have been a congenial person in spite of his evangelistic intensity because he was popular among young people.

During the height of the revival years that swept central and western New York, excitement was high. Business was often suspended. Revival was the chief conversation in shops and on the streets, even in the taverns. Many places closed in the evening so that all could attend the services. The revival in Rome, N.Y., continued for nearly a year after Finney had left town.

The impact of the Finney years is difficult to overstate. Entire communities were changed under the spiritual spell of his revivals. And long after Finney had left upstate New York for a pastorate in New York City, and later as a professor and then pastor in Oberlin College, the spirit of revival continued. No one can deny the important role of evangelist Charles G. Finney in the development and use of the public invitation, particularly relating to the anxious seat and the inquiry sessions.

Charles G. Finney's Time Line

1792

Charles G. Finney was born in Warren, Conn., the son of a gardener who was a veteran of the American Revolution. The family of seven children moved to Oneida County, New York, just south of the fertile Mohawk Valley, in 1794 when Charles was only two years old.

1818

After teaching school in New Jersey for two years, Charles Finney entered the profession of law by moving to Adams, N.Y., where he worked and studied in the law firm of Judge Benjamin Wright. He was 26 years old.

Two years after beginning his studies with Judge Wright,

Charles Finney finished the reading list, passed the examinations, and settled down to a successful practice.

1821

Charles Finney, the young lawyer, made a decision to settle the question of his soul's salvation at once. He had a spiritual crisis on Wednesday, October 10, followed by an unusual experience that evening, "when it seemed as if I met the Lord Jesus Christ face-to-face."

1824

Three years after his conversion, Charles G. Finney was licensed to preach in the Presbyterian church.

1830

In a Rochester, N.Y., revival that lasted more than six months, Finney established the anxious seat for the first time in a systematic approach to his invitation and continued using it thereafter.

1832

Broken in health and physically exhausted, Finney accepted a call to pastor the Second Free Presbyterian Church in New York City, which met in the 3,000-seat, remodeled Chatham Street Theater. Finney's salary was $1,500 a year with two months off for conducting revivals. Frustration over the doctrine and the policies of the Presbyterian church led Finney to accept a call to pastor the Broadway Tabernacle in 1834. It was here he preached his famous series of messages on revivals that were published under the title *Lectures on Revivals of Religion.* This was the most significant single work of his career and one of his great contributions to the cause of evangelism.

1835-75

Finney served successively as professor, president, and pastor at Oberlin College. He was approaching 70 years of age when he accepted the pastorate of the College Church, which he held for more than a decade. He owned his own tent and held a protracted meeting in the community at least once each year. His circular tent was 100 feet in diameter and was equipped with a large streamer at the top of the center pole that read, "Holiness unto the Lord."

1875

Charles G. Finney died at 83 years of age, having given all of his life, after conversion, to the further growth and development of revivalism. Many have said that the anxious seat was a symbol of all his "new measures." And it was his new measures that brought the camp meeting into town.

Finney's Conversion

One of Finney's strongest continuing motivations for revivalism was his own conversion. The depth of this spiritual experience, coupled with the legal mind he developed in the offices of Judge Wright, plus his own strong individualism in seeking answers, became the three-legged anvil on which he hammered out the meaning of the Scriptures and their application to Christian experience.

Without formal theological training, his legal mind-set made him seek for biblical precedents and confirming witness in human experiences to fortify preaching. For instance, the criticism of disorderliness in his services was met by Finney who cited Pentecost as a precedent, when many outside people thought the Christians were drunk with new wine. He also rejected the Calvinistic idea of a totally depraved, helpless person who could only wait passively to be brought to life by the Holy Spirit through a logical appeal to the Bible. In Finney's logic the Bible would not call for repentance and faith unless man had some control over the exercise of his own repentance and the stirring up of his own faith.

As the legal mind of John Calvin had led him to the idea of man's total and absolute depravity and spiritual helplessness, the same kind of legal mind led Charles G. Finney to assert personal responsibility in the matter of salvation based on the truth in prevenient grace. The mind-set of a lawyer and his strong personal commitment to finding his own answers were distinct elements in the dramatic story of Finney's conversion.

Until Finney moved to Adams, his life had been virtually void of any kind of religious training or religious interests. He had never heard a prayer in his home, and he had only attended a few church services during his childhood and teen years. He said later in his memoirs, "I was almost as ignorant of religion as a heathen. I had been brought up mostly in the woods. I had little regard for the Sabbath and had no definite knowledge of religious truth." However, Rev. George Gale, pastor of the Presbyterian church in Adams, needed a choir director and drafted young Charles Finney. In his assignment, Finney was expected to attend all church services, including prayer meeting, in the Presbyterian church.

Finney developed an unusual interest in the Bible by tracing the Scripture references of his study in elementary law. "I found the old authors frequently quoting the Scriptures, and referring especially to the Mosaic institutes, as authority for many of the great principles of common law. This excited my curiosity so much that I went and purchased a Bible."

Reading the Bible, attending church regularly, talking with the pastor about his sermons, singing religious songs, and meeting church people in nonthreatening social relationships brought young lawyer Finney into an entirely new way of thinking and feeling about religion. Also, Finney had become interested in a young lady, Lydia Andrews, whom he had met when she was 18 years old. Her interest in salvation was a factor in his conversion.

With his lawyer's mind-set, Finney saw a glaring contradiction in the theological position of Pastor Gale. "If he preached repentance, he must be sure before he sat down to leave the impression on his people that they could not repent. If he called them to believe, he must be sure to inform them, that until their nature was changed by the Holy Spirit, faith was impossible to them. And so his orthodoxy was a perfect snare to himself and his hearers."

Another contradiction and stumbling block to Finney's conversion were the unanswered prayers from Rev. Gale week by week. He prayed, but as far as Finney could tell, nothing ever happened. However, Charles Finney finally came to the place in his study of the Bible that made it impossible for him to continue denying the gospel. In spite of inconsistencies in unanswered prayers, unresolved theological issues, and unsatisfactory sermons, Finney finally came to comprehend the gospel as taught in the Bible. As Mendell Taylor says in his book *Exploring Evangelism,* "Finney came to believe that the gospel was presented in the Scriptures as an absolute authority in a person's life."

Finally on a Sunday evening in October 1821, Charles Finney decided to "settle the question of his soul's salvation at once." On the following Wednesday morning he took a walk in the woods for private time to struggle with two facts he saw in the Scriptures. (1) The Atonement was complete in the death and resurrection of Jesus and did not require our righteousness to make it real. And, (2) faith was a voluntary trust and not an intellectual state. Therefore, consent to give up sin and accept Christ was all it took to be converted. Salvation was more simple than he had ever dreamed.

During the evening following his morning walk in the woods, Finney had a most unusual vision: Jesus Christ became so real to him it was not until much later that he realized his vision was only a mental state and not a physical experience. "In this state I was taught the doctrine of justification by faith as a present experience."

Finney's conversion had a profound effect on Pastor Gale's Presbyterian church. The whole community heard the word that Finney was converted, because many had all but given up on him including his pastor. One young person was heard to say, "If you convert Finney, I will believe there is something to religion." His pastor later confessed that he had stopped asking the people to pray for the conversion of Charles Finney because he felt as if the young lawyer was a hopeless case.

Most of the young people associated with Finney were already converted. But they threw themselves into revival in a new way when lawyer Finney was converted. They joined him in witnessing to people on the streets, in the shops, and wherever Finney and his cohorts could get anyone to listen. After a series of meetings, 63 people joined the church.

Charles G. Finney was a young lawyer on his way. He had the oratorical style and force to make himself someone to be reckoned with in politics. But events in the week of October 7, 1821, changed everything. Finney moved from the courtroom to the church house and from the bar of justice to the anxious seat.

The next day following his conversion, Finney went to his office at the regular time. His first client was a deacon from the church who came to talk about his case, which was on the docket for ten o'clock that morning. Finney listened to him and then said, "Deacon, I have a retainer from the Lord Jesus Christ to plead His cause, and I cannot plead yours. . . . You must go and get someone else to attend your lawsuit. I could not do it."

The deacon dropped his head and made a quick exit but not to hire another lawyer; overwhelmed by Finney, he moved immediately toward settling his case outside court and turned to engage in prayer for himself.

Finney no longer had any desire to practice law. He seemed dead to worldly pleasures and amusements that had previously held him hostage. His whole mind was taken up with Jesus and the issue of personal salvation. Secular matters now seemed of little consequence.

The significance of Finney's conversion story is the strong motivation it provided for many years of intensive endeavor to bring this same experience to as many persons as he possibly could. No one could hope for salvation without an experience with Christ. Finney believed this so sincerely that every time a conversion occurred under his preaching, he felt he had literally rescued a soul from the brink of hell.

Charles Finney's Theology of Evangelism

After a radical conversion experience that included rejection of his pastor's theology, a deep searching of the Scriptures for the meaning of the Christian gospel, and a highly compelling religious experience, no one could expect Charles Finney to simply restate the theology of the Presbyterian church without questioning its tenets. Finney had not purchased a Bible until he was nearly 30 years old, and he declined formal schooling as preparation for the ministry so that he could begin preaching immediately. If he were not going to Princeton as other aspiring young Presbyterian preachers did, it was a natural consequence for him to study theology with his pastor, G. W. Gale, as he had studied law with Judge Benjamin Wright.

Finney and his pastor had numerous dead ends in their theological conversations with each other. Gale preached a necessity of conversion but told the people they could do nothing but wait for the Holy Spirit to convert them. In his memoirs, Finney said, "Often when I left Mr. Gale, I would go to my room and spend a long time on my knees over my Bible. I had nowhere to go but directly to the Bible, and to the philosophy or workings of my own mind, as revealed in consciousness." Finney was not satisfied with Gale's teachings or with the orthodox Calvinistic books that filled his pastor's library.

However, there was a bright side to the contention these men had with each other on theological matters. Finney said, "At first I found myself unable to receive his Calvinistic views; and then gradually I formed views of my own in opposition to them, which appeared to be unequivocally taught in the Bible." When Charles Finney was finally licensed to preach, he had not yet read the Westminster Confession of Faith for the Presbyterian church. When he did finally read it, he was aghast. "When I came to read the Confession of Faith . . . I was absolutely ashamed of it. I could not feel any respect for a document that would undertake to impose on mankind such dogmas as those, sustained, for the most part, by passages of Scripture that were totally irrelevant."

As the studies went on, Gale was more and more on the defensive. During a revival some two years later, Gale told Finney that he "thanked God that he had had no influence with me, to lead me to adopt his views; that I should have been ruined as a minister if he had prevailed."

Finney's theology resulted in some inconsistencies because of his efforts to adapt to Calvinistic terminology by redefining its terms. James E. Johnson, in his study on the theology of Finney, concludes, "He probably felt more comfortable in the pulpit than in the study, for he possessed a power over a crowd that was somewhat diminished when he put his ideas in print." However, the theology of Finney, like that of Wesley and Asbury, was hammered out on the anvil of practical experience in saving souls.

As a lasting contribution, Finney brought a great host of pioneer people to Christ and into the church who were well on their way toward indifference and rejection of orthodox Christianity. The message he preached was plain and straightforward. As McLoughlin points out in his book *Modern Revivalism,* Pastor Gale abandoned his crippling Calvinistic views for the free will in Finney's theology, and it was not many years until western New York had followed suit.

William Walzer, in his Ph.D. dissertation at the University of Chicago, says of Finney's message, "Conversion is primarily the sinner's own act. It is true that in a sense the one who speaks to him converts, and in a sense God converts; but the actual decision is that of the convert, freely made. If sinners say they are waiting for God to convert them, they are simply making excuses."

In his *Lectures to Professing Christians* Finney explains how salvation is the responsibility of the sinner. "Your pardon is ready, made out and sealed with the broad seal of heaven; and the blank will be filled up and the gracious pardon delivered as soon as by one act of faith you receive

Jesus Christ as He is offered in the gospel." In *Gospel Themes* Finney says, "If you cannot make up your mind to discard sin and obey God, you may as well make up your mind to go to hell! There is no alternative."

The strict Calvinists said that man could do nothing to gain salvation until the Holy Spirit converted him, and they accused Finney of leaving God out of the picture. However, Finney believed that the Holy Spirit performed the function of persuasion. The Holy Spirit held the truth up to a man in the hope that he would see, understand, and act.

Finney believed that truth in the form of intellectual abstractions was not enough to move the will. He believed the mind had to be brought under a degree of emotion to influence the will. This was the value of a religious revival as compared with mere religious discussion. It is evident that all of Finney's theology was subordinated to his revival purposes.

Gradually Finney developed the concept of sanctification as a second element in his view of salvation. His idea of entire sanctification grew naturally out of his revivalistic activity.

During the years of 1824-32, when Finney was a full-time traveling evangelist, his residence in a community would often keep the spiritual tide high for as long as six months or more after he left. However, the task of assimilating the converts, bringing them into the life of the church, and preventing backsliding was left to the resident pastor.

It was not until he had been at Oberlin and had worked over the issue of sanctification with President Asa Mahan, and not until after he had experienced a deeply moving religious encounter during a stay in Boston, that Finney declared fully the doctrine of sanctification.

During his pastorate at the Broadway Tabernacle in New York City, Finney delivered 25 lectures to professing Christians and devoted the "last 9 of these to the doctrine of entire sanctification." On another occasion Finney said he emphasized the doctrine of entire sanctification because "after 10 years as a revivalist, I am fully convinced that converts would die, that the standard of piety would never be elevated, that revivals would become more and more superficial, and finally cease, unless something effectual was done to elevate the standard of holiness in the church."

As Wesley and Asbury had done before him, Finney reduced Christian perfection to a matter of the will to love God and to love our neighbor. Charles Finney was greatly impressed by the doctrine of the Methodists and recommended Wesley's work on Christian perfection to all his people.

Finney's preaching, like his theology, was directed toward personal action. Finney told his audiences, "I am not talking about everybody else; but I mean you, and you, and you."

Finney wanted people to see the light on salvation and then do something about it. In his *Memoirs* Finney told of his experience in a certain city where he was well received by the people for some three consecutive Sundays. "But after all, I did not come there to please, but to bring them to repentance; that it mattered not to me how well they were pleased with my preaching, if after all they rejected my Master." Finney put the matter of salvation squarely before the people for a decision and asked those to stand who had made up their minds to become Christians, while those who had resolved not to accept the gospel were asked to remain seated.

In bewilderment, everyone remained seated.

After a moment Finney said to them, "Then you are committed. You have taken your stand. You have rejected Christ and His gospel; and you are witnesses one against the other, and God is witness to you all."

The people were outraged as they walked out, except for one old deacon who came forward to assure Charles Finney that he had done well. Threats were made to tar and feather him. But the next evening the people were all back at the meetings again, and for 1½ hours Finney preached, assuming they were all committed against the Lord.

Finney's method was personal and straightforward. "I talked to the people as I would to a jury." The great length of his sermons was due in part to the repetition that he felt was necessary to convince the entire congregation. As he watched the faces of the people, he never hesitated to go back and repeat his arguments if he thought they were puzzled about what he was explaining. Much of the time, Finney was so natural in the pulpit and his delivery was so conversational that people accustomed to a ministerial tone said that it did not seem like preaching. Finney's theology of evangelism may have contained its inconsistencies and, like all theology, raised new questions while answering others. But no one could deny the fact that the message of full salvation, as Finney saw it in the Bible, was clearly explained night by night. The people might not believe the gospel, but no one ever doubted that Finney did.

Mendell Taylor, in *Exploring Evangelism*, quotes Finney in a beautiful summary of the evangelist's theology of evangelism: "The doctrines preached in promoting that revival [Gouverneur, New York, 1825] were those I have preached everywhere. The total moral, voluntary depravity of unregenerate man; the necessity of a radical change of heart, through the truth, by the agency of the Holy Ghost; repentance, faith, justification by faith, sanctification by faith; persistence in holiness as a condition of salvation; indeed all the distinctive doctrines of the Gospel were stated and set forth with as much clearness, and point, and power, as were possible to me under the circumstances."

New Measures and the Anxious Seat

If the revivalism of Charles G. Finney was motivated by his own radical conversion experience and his clear concept of the gospel as he saw it revealed in the New Testament, then his revival methods grew out of his own individualism, which had been honed on life in a pioneer country. Since Finney believed in his own experiences, anything that helped the revival was soon incorporated into his system of procedures. These ideas were called "new measures" and were the source of much contention and criticism from the people committed to old, Calvinistic orthodoxy. For instance, he believed in setting dates for revival. This brought down the wrath of the old-line Calvinists who asked how anyone could tell God when there would be a revival. God brought revival in His own good time, and it was totally presumptuous and arrogant for any man to set a date. Finney simply answered that revival was promised and would come whenever Christians met the requisites described in the Bible.

Another new measure was his focus on the prayer of faith, based on Bible promises and therefore not to be denied. He believed in a highly emotional kind of prayer. He encouraged women to pray publicly, a totally new measure among the churches where he ministered. Prayer meetings lasted for many hours, sometimes all night. Finney prayed in homes, in the woods, in his room, and in the pulpit. Some people maintained that his praying was more effective in bringing people to conversion than his sermons were in bringing them to a conviction of sin.

Early in his ministry Finney was joined by Father Nash, an eccentric old preacher who exercised the prayer of faith. He was a man who prayed without ceasing. He kept long lists of the names of sinners. They said his private prayers could be heard a half mile away. Finney would ask Father Nash to pray with a small group while he was in the pulpit preaching. Some reported that the voice of Father Nash could be heard in the dramatic pauses that punctuated the sermons of Finney. The method was effective.

Finney prayed for sinners in public by name. Sometimes he even named their vices. This made some people angry; others requested that their names be included in these public prayers. Either way, the whole idea was a new measure. Finney's informal, street language used in prayer was to some irreverent.

Songs and hymns were not used to any great extent in Finney's revivals. Finney once said, "I never knew a singing revival to amount to much. Its tendency is to do away with all deep feeling." He often opened a service with the singing of a single hymn and then used the rest of the evening for praying and preaching.

But there was one new measure that became the symbol for all the others: the anxious seat.

During his six-month protracted meeting in Rochester, N.Y., Charles Finney first introduced the practice and technique of asking persons under conviction of sin to come forward to a place in the first pew that became known as the anxious seat or the anxious bench. He had previously preferred the raising of hands, or standing, as an indication of need, but found the greatest obstacle for many people to overcome was their fear of being known as an anxious inquirer. Finney knew by intuition that the best way to overcome this fear was to compel people to make an open and public stand for Christ. He compared coming to the anxious seat to baptism in the Early Church. It was a public commitment of being on the Lord's side.

Closely related to the anxious seat was the anxious meeting. When persons did not obtain a satisfactory relationship with Christ at the anxious seat, they were encouraged, as inquirers, to attend an anxious meeting, usually held in an adjacent room. The anxious meeting was held for the purpose of giving instruction to those who were in different stages of conviction. Questions were answered. Every effort was made to bring each seeker face-to-face with the great question of unqualified acceptance of the Atonement for salvation. As Mendell Taylor points out, the place of this meeting was eventually called the inquiry room.

Opposition to the anxious seat and the inquiry room mainly came from their theological significance. Old-school Calvinists were unwilling to admit that individuals possessed the power to submit to God for salvation. In their view, conversion could only follow regeneration, a mysterious process by which the heart of the elect was changed by God himself with or without man's cooperation. Thus they would never urge men to repent until God had transformed their desires according to His sovereign grace.

However, Finney assumed that the perverse will of the sinner was the only barrier keeping him from being a possessor of the divine promises. He believed that the purpose of revival was to push matters to an issue on personal salvation, and the anxious seat was a good means to this end.

William Oscar Thompson, Jr., in his dissertation, makes a point on the swiftness with which the anxious seat became the invitational method of the Baptists. He cites records from local congregations who held protracted meetings and used the anxious seat after 1825. They believed that the anxious seat, like anything else that was good, was subject to abuse, but that was no reason why its prudent use should be abandoned.

In his autobiography, Jacob Knapp, an early-day Baptist minister, gives five reasons for using the anxious seat: (1) It serves as a test of character. (2) It is a public committal. (3) It is a convenient way of making a public acknowledgment of our need of Christ. (4) Such an example is an encouragement to other convicted souls. (5) It is an encouragement to the minister and the church.

New methods always follow a shift in theology. With Charles G. Finney came a shift from the Calvinistic ideas brought with the pioneers from New England to the new measures that tilted toward personal responsibility for both repentance and faith. The result was the experience of personal salvation. The aggressive, uninhibited Finney pressed his theology and his new measures until the results they produced forced capitulation of pastors and churches throughout the Empire State and beyond.

Due to his great fame as an evangelist, his far-flung publications, and his direct influence on most of the itinerant evangelists who followed him, Charles G. Finney was without question a leading contributor to the use of the public invitation as a method of evangelism and particularly the development and widespread use of the anxious seat. The altar was just one small step away.

9

Phineas F. Bresee and the Glory of the Altar

PHINEAS F. BRESEE, founder of the Los Angeles First Church of the Nazarene in 1895, was first and foremost a pastor-evangelist. He was 70 years old when the Nazarenes elected him general superintendent by acclamation at Pilot Point, Tex., in 1908. He did not resign his Los Angeles pastorate until 1911, when he was 73 years old. Whatever else may be said about his ministry, he was a pastor with the heart of an evangelist.

Bresee was born a Methodist and was converted in a Methodist revival under the preaching of his own pastor. Since preachers tend to preach like the men preached when they were converted, it is no small wonder Bresee became a pastor-evangelist. He was following in the steps of his pastor, Brother Smith, the man who won him to the Lord. Although Bresee had already been a Methodist pastor for 19 years when the former Presbyterian evangelist, Charles G. Finney, died, there is no mention of him by Bresee. He was apparently influenced primarily by the methods and theology of Asbury and his successors.

Within months after Bresee was converted, he preached on a Sunday afternoon at a place called The Hemlocks in western New York. His text from Ps. 124:7 prepared the way for a conversion-centered sermon, which he began with the story of creation, moved through time to his conversion, and then concluded with the end of the world and the judgment, all in 20 minutes.

Bresee was appointed to his first Methodist circuit in Iowa when he was 18 years old, using the exhorter's license given him by his pastor back in New York State. With the exception of two brief intervals as presiding elder (district superintendent) and one year with the Peniel Mission in Los Angeles, P. F. Bresee served 55 years in pulpits where he was called pastor.

The death of Bishop Asbury and the birth of Phineas Bresee were separated by 22 years in which Methodism matured as the strong evangelical voice in America. Surely the joyous, happy, positive ways of the Methodists fully obtained in the mind and ministry of their illustrious son Phineas in upstate New York, later in Iowa, and still later in California. The public invitation was widely accepted and fully systematized in most evangelical churches by the time Bresee was born. And the Methodist mourner's bench had become the Methodist altar, universally accepted in the Methodist church by the time Bresee became a circuit rider in Iowa. Among Methodists the invitation was warmly referred to as the altar call; and the sequence of invitation—seekers coming forward, united prayer, victory, testimonies, and shouting —was referred to as the altar service. The pulpit, Communion table, and altar rail had become integral parts of Methodist evangelism, each sustaining the other in a symbiotic relationship.

During Bresee's 55-year tenure as a pastor-evangelist, the altar and the altar call were central in Methodist worship. The focus on the altar affected (1) the nature of the service including the music, (2) the character and purpose of the sermon, and (3) the accepted forms in worship and evangelism. Proof of the central focus on the altar comes in the way the altar is thoroughly woven into the total fabric of

Bresee's ministry. Remove the altar, and Bresee's ministry comes unraveled. He was unself-conscious about the altar and the altar call. The pulpit and the altar were opposite sides of the same coin. The final effectiveness of a year's ministry for Bresee depended on what had happened in the name of the Lord at the altar. It was his concept of the altar and the public altar call that Bresee translated into the Nazarene altar after 1895, beginning in Los Angeles.

Phineas Bresee's Time Line

1838

Phineas F. Bresee was born on the 31st day of December, 1838, in the community of Franklin, Delaware County, New York. He was born in a log house about five miles from the village of Franklin. Later in life when he felt the need for a middle name, he chose Franklin in honor of the town where he was born.

1856

Phineas Bresee was converted in February 1856 during a protracted meeting in the little Methodist church where his parents were members. The pastor came to the store where Phineas was working and spoke to him about his soul. This was the means of bringing him under conviction, and he determined he would go to the meeting that night and seek salvation. "I went and he preached. I thought he never would get through and give me a chance to go to the altar, but he did, finally, after preaching and exhorting. Nobody had been to the altar up to that time in the meeting, but he gave me a chance, and I went immediately, and others followed." His conversion came the following Sunday. (Unless otherwise indicated, quotes in this chapter come from *A Prince in Israel*, by Girvin. Two other helpful sources are Brickley's *Man of the Morning* and Timothy Smith's *Called unto Holiness*, vol. 1.)

1857

The Bresee family moved from New York to Iowa. The Iowa farm was 6 or 7 miles west of Millersburg on the main road that ran directly through the state. The next town, 14 miles west of their farm, was Montezuma. Bresee began to preach immediately on arrival in his new home.

1860

At the close of his two-year pastorate in Pella, Phineas Bresee, who had become engaged by letter to Maria E. Hibbard, went back to New York for the wedding.

1864

Bresee was appointed presiding elder at 26 years of age, after a successful pastorate on the circuit that centered in Grinnell. This was followed by an appointment to the Galesburg circuit. He began a revival in that circuit in October that lasted until spring, filling the largest schoolhouses in the area. As Bresee said, "The Lord gave me the country." Like Wesley and Asbury before him, Phineas Bresee redeemed the long rides across the prairie by learning how to read in motion.

1866

During a revival in Chariton, Phineas Bresee was sanctified at his own altar on a stormy night with the mercury 20 degrees below zero and with a very small congregation.

1883

After a series of successful pastorates, including the Broadway Church in Council Bluffs, Dr. Bresee took his family from Iowa to southern California. They made the trip in a Union Pacific Railroad car, which they fitted up with beds, curtains, and other amenities. It was a camping trip on rails. A few friends who also wanted to go to California were permitted to ride in the same car.

"The trip was, in every way, full of interest and picturesqueness. Sometimes our car was hitched to the express train, sometimes to a freight train, and sometimes it was sidetracked. Occasionally we were left over two or three hours in some village, and that gave us fine opportunities for observation and pleasure."

It took eight days for the journey from Council Bluffs to Los Angeles, where the Bresee family arrived on Saturday afternoon, August 26, 1883. The next morning they attended the First Methodist Church. When he arrived at the door, an usher hurriedly took Bresee to the pastor's study, where he was told they were expecting him to preach. He did.

Los Angeles was a city of 20,000 people when Phineas Bresee was appointed pastor of the First Methodist Episcopal Church by Bishop Warren. Here Dr. Bresee, for the first time in his ministry, worked with a class of fully sanctified people.

1886

Dr. Bresee was appointed pastor of the First Methodist Church in Pasadena. When Dr. Bresee was asked what he was going to do at Pasadena, he replied that, by the grace of God, he would "make a fire that would reach heaven." During four years, Dr. Bresee took 1,000 members into the church.

1891

Bresee was appointed presiding elder of the Los Angeles District. "The importance of this year of service can scarcely be overestimated in my life, because of so many things entering into it, which were finally influential in determining the course of my career in the work of holiness, and the future great Nazarene movement."

1892

Dr. Bresee began to feel strong opposition to holiness from the Methodist bishops. "If I had known more when I came to this coast, and had had experience and sense, I could have swept the whole of Methodism into holiness. It was not set against it enough to prevent me from putting my hands on everything in Methodism in southern California, and drawing it into holiness; but I did not know enough. I neither had the experience nor the general ministerial wisdom to do it. I am very sorry."

1895

The Church of the Nazarene was organized on the third Sunday of October for "the declared purpose of preaching holiness, and carrying the gospel to the poor." The organization was finally consummated with 135 charter members.

1897

Bresee organized the Church of the Nazarene in Berkeley and Oakland, the first reach of the Nazarene movement beyond Los Angeles. A second church in Los Angeles was organized the same year.

1900

During the assembly of the Church of the Nazarene, held at the old Tabernacle on Los Angeles Street in October, "Dr. Bresee presided, and a half hour was spent in prayer, after which there was preaching, followed by a testimony meeting, and an altar service." During that same year, Dr. Bresee suffered a serious accident when his buggy was hit by a streetcar in Los Angeles.

1903

On Friday night, March 20, a great march was planned from the old Tabernacle to the new church at Sixth and Wall streets. Girvin says, "The occasion drew together a vast concourse of people, estimated to have been at least 10,000 in number. When we had entered the new building, it was packed from top to bottom, at least 2,500 persons being in it; the great crowds on Sixth and Wall streets did not seem to be diminished."

1907

The Association of Pentecostal Churches of America from the East became associated with the Church of the Nazarene in a merger resulting in the Pentecostal Church of the Nazarene. The two groups voted unanimously on both the merger and the name.

1908

The Holiness Church of Christ, representing more than 3,000 members in the southern states, decided to unite with the Pentecostal Church of the Nazarene and requested a joint session with the General Assembly of the Pentecostal Church of the Nazarene be held at Pilot Point, Tex., on October 8. The sessions were held in a tent seating 1,000. The motion for merger carried unanimously by a standing vote, amid great enthusiasm.

1911

The General Assembly of the Pentecostal Church of the Nazarene was held in Nashville, with host J. O. McClurkan and the people of the Pentecostal Mission. Denominational membership and property values in the Pentecostal Church of the Nazarene had almost doubled in three years since Pilot Point. The Nashville daily paper said that no religious gathering had so affected the city since the great meeting of Moody and Sankey. From the first session there was a tide of salvation. Many were saved and sanctified. The first day of the General Assembly was devoted primarily to worship. Evangelistic services were held every evening with great congregations meeting in the Ryman Auditorium, erected for evangelist Sam Jones.

1915

Dr. P. F. Bresee died on Saturday afternoon, November 13. At his funeral the male quartet from the Nazarene University sang "Lead, Kindly Light." Pastor C. E. Cornell gave a luminous exposition of Ps. 37:37: "Mark the perfect man, and behold the upright: for the end of that man is peace." Dr. H. Orton Wiley, president of the Nazarene University, closed the service with a few words and pronounced the benediction.

There is an interesting story in Donald P. Brickley's book *Man of the Morning,* about Dr. Bresee's custom of standing at the door of the church each Sunday morning to greet people as they arrived. He continued this practice even when the church became very large, shaking hands with more than 1,000 people. One day he gave assistance to an elderly lady, greeting her by name as she entered the church. She thanked him and remarked that she hoped he would be at heaven's gate to greet her when she arrived. Dr. Bresee suggested that she would not need any assistance when she got to heaven. "But," he said, "I'll meet you just inside the Eastern Gate."

When Rev. I. G. Martin heard this story, he wrote the words and music to the song "The Eastern Gate" and dedicated it to Dr. Phineas Franklin Bresee.

> I will meet you in the morning,
> Just inside the Eastern Gate.
> Then be ready, faithful pilgrim,
> Lest with you it be too late.
>
> If you hasten off to glory,
> Linger near the Eastern Gate,
> For I'm coming in the morning;
> So you'll not have long to wait.

Dr. Bresee's Theology of Evangelism

Dr. Bresee's theology of evangelism developed both from three personal religious experiences and from his consuming concern for the biblical experience of entire sanctification and the life of holiness. The three religious events that furnished substance and structure for his work as pastor-evangelist were (1) his conversion in Davenport, N.Y., (2) his experience of sanctification at his own altar in Chariton, Iowa, and (3) his ball-of-fire experience in the parsonage at Los Angeles.

Bresee's conversion in his late teens was a natural step in the Christian nurturing of a solid Methodist family who extolled the virtues of Methodism and its leaders. With Bresee, conversion and a call to preach were closely related. After his pastor talked with him in the store where he worked, young Phineas decided he would tend to the matter of his salvation.

On Friday night in the revival, with the local pastor preaching, Bresee was impatient and could scarcely wait for the sermon to end and the altar call to begin. He was the first seeker at the altar during the protracted meeting, although others followed his lead. In the class meeting on Sunday after church, Phineas Bresee was converted. He entered Christian service immediately. Three months later he received his first Methodist license as an exhorter. And within a year, the family had moved to Iowa, and Bresee was in the full-time ministry as a pastor-evangelist.

Ten years after his conversion, Bresee was serving the Methodist congregation in Chariton, Iowa. His outspoken sermons on worldliness, as he saw it, kept the church upset. As he said, "They seemed peculiarly adapted to not liking it." Furthermore, he was plagued with his own continuing doubts and general lack of spiritual vitality.

Writing about his experience later, Bresee said, "I had come to the point where I seemingly could not go on. My religion did not meet my needs. I was ignorant of my own condition. I did not understand . . . carnality." Things came to a head on a snowy night during the midwinter protracted meeting when the temperature was 20 below zero and few people were in the service.

The pastor-evangelist had a hard time preaching and an even harder time during the altar call. The people who were gathered around the stove at the back of the church were not inclined to move to the altar even though Pastor Bresee went back to them in search of a seeker. Unsuccessful in his quest, he turned toward the altar, and "in some way, it seemed to me, that this was my time. I threw myself down across the altar and began to pray for myself. The Lord helped me, drew me and impelled me, as I cried to him that night. He seemed to open heaven, and gave me, as I believe, the baptism with the Holy Ghost, though I did not know . . . what I needed, or what I prayed for. . . . No one got sanctified but myself."

Soon after Dr. Bresee transplanted his ministry from Iowa to California, he felt a deep need for a reassuring experience. Los Angeles was a city of 20,000, and there was much work to be done in this newly developing country. Bresee's First Methodist Church had between 300 and 400 members. For the first time in his ministry he had found "a class of fully sanctified people." Instinctively, his spirit was allied with theirs. "While they must have known I was not in the clear enjoyment of the blessing, they seemed to appreciate whatever efforts I could and did make in assisting them in the work of holiness. They were very kind and gentle. They doubtless prayed much for me, but they did not pray at me."

Pastor Bresee was like Isaiah in the Temple (chap. 6), waiting for a sending experience that would give him a point of reference and a compelling sense of spiritual readiness for his task.

Writing later about the second year of his pastorate in the First Methodist Church of Los Angeles, Dr. Bresee said, "I began to be awakened to the deep necessities of my own heart. This realization grew more and more intense, until my heart cry began to go out to God for the mighty grace that was adequate for all my needs."

After some days of almost constant prayer, Bresee sat alone one evening near the open door of the front parlor, enjoying the cool of the day. Bresee looked out the door, continuing to pray as he apparently watched the sunset.

Then, from the azure came an indescribable ball of condensed light, descending toward him like a meteor. As it drew closer, there seemed to be a voice saying, "Swallow it! Swallow it!" An instant later the ball of fire fell on his lips. Dr. Bresee tried to swallow it but with limited success. "It seemed to me that I swallowed only a little of it, although it felt like fire on my lips; the burning sensation did not leave them for several days."

Dr. Bresee said, "While all of this would be nothing of itself, there came . . . into my heart and being, a transformed condition of life and blessing, and unction and glory which I had never known before. . . . I have said very little relative to this; but there came into my ministry a new element of spiritual life and power." With Isaiah, Pastor Bresee could cry, "Here am I; send me." He had felt the touch of the fire from off God's altar.

After Dr. Bresee's ball-of-fire experience, people in Los Angeles First Methodist Church "began to come into the blessing of full salvation." The church began to grow. And by the end of Bresee's third year the spirit of love and joy was still exploding in First Church, and the membership had nearly doubled.

It is not difficult to understand why Dr. Bresee's theology of evangelism was based on personal religious experiences. His conversion in New York, his sanctification in Iowa, and the outpouring of enabling grace in California were vital signposts in his Christian pilgrimage.

* * *

The second major factor in Bresee's theology of evangelism was a strong commitment to the doctrine and experience of sanctification and a life of holiness. Bresee's separation from the Methodist denomination, where he had served all his adult life, was over the growing opposition to holiness among the bishops and the more sophisticated laymen in strategic churches. After an honest try for an assignment among the poor, Phineas Bresee was ultimately rejected. His final option for preaching holiness among the poor was to lay down his Methodist ministry and leave the annual conference with no assignment.

"When I laid it down that day, it seemed to me I laid down everything . . . I had loved and labored for. My heart was full of almost unbearable sadness. The night was spent in much prayer, and with many tears." In the morning when Bresee arose, he picked up his Bible in the sitting room and asked the Lord to give him a message. In Isa. 66:5 he read, "Your brethren that hated you, that cast you out . . . he shall appear to your joy, and they shall be ashamed."

On the following Sunday, Bresee preached in Redlands, and 75 persons were at the altar seeking the Lord, most of them for entire sanctification. The hurt was not gone, but healing was under way. More important, the man of the morning could now give himself to holiness evangelism. He was almost 57 years old.

The first printed notice announcing the opening of Dr. Bresee's new work on October 6, 1895, at 11 A.M. on South Main Street in Los Angeles, made his purpose clear: "the spreading of the doctrine and the experience of Christian holiness." Two weeks later the congregation was organized with 86 men and women who stood to pledge their support to the work of the Church of the Nazarene "with the avowed purpose of preaching holiness, and carrying the gospel to the poor." The charter eventually included 135 names. Under the leadership of a pastor-evangelist, people were being saved and sanctified week by week with a total membership of 350 by the end of the first year. Their small building was expanded to seat 800.

The name Nazarene had special meaning to these people in First Church. Dr. Bresee said they "went out to follow in the footsteps of Him whose name they bear—to bring comfort to the sorrowing, help to the downcast, a message of hope to the brokenhearted, and the gospel of peace to lives burdened with sin." However, by the end of their second year the scope of Nazarene evangelism had expanded to include "hungry hearts and neglected lives in homes that the world does not call poor, . . . to go wherever lives are burdened with sin."

The scope of the call of Nazarenes was expanded, but their focus on the altar was still singular. In March of 1898, Dr. Bresee wrote, "Nearly every service is crowned with the salvation of sinners and the sanctification of believers."

Everything in Dr. Bresee's church was geared to holiness evangelism. The Sunday schedule included (1) an early morning prayer meeting, (2) Sunday School, (3) morning worship, (4) family dinner at the church, (5) an afternoon holiness meeting, (6) followed by visitation in the neighborhood, (7) and a lively night service, (8) preceded by a street meeting. The Los Angeles streetcars, after nine o'clock on Sunday nights, must have been filled with Nazarene families carrying empty hampers while their hearts were brimming with spiritual satisfaction.

The young people's meeting was held on Friday nights with "many cases of triumphant conversion and sanctification." Company E, led by Mrs. Lucy Knott, was devoted to the salvation of young ladies, while the Brotherhood of St. Stephen was a zealous group of young men.

Under the leadership of their pastor-evangelist, the entire resources in Los Angeles First Church of the Nazarene were mobilized for recruiting people who were led in the experiences of conversion and entire sanctification and grounded in the holiness way. Dr. Bresee's goal was to make every new convert a soul winner.

Bresee's Focus on the Altar

The altar, which served as the focal point of Dr. Bresee's ministry in the Methodist church, was even more important to him in the Church of the Nazarene. He usually preached a short sermon and sat down at the conclusion as the people began to sing an old hymn. Then the pastor-evangelist would go out into the congregation "and reap for the altar." As the crowds grew, Dr. Bresee often used laymen who met with him before the service to assist in this one-on-one invitation. When the seekers had come forward, "they would rally at the altar in the old Methodist fashion and pray with the penitents until they got through."

However, Dr. Bresee used the Nazarene altar in a variety of ways not related directly to evangelism. He sometimes started services, especially on weekdays when the crowds were smaller, with prayers at the altar by everyone. After an especially glorious service he raised the sign "Victory" above the altar as a continuing reminder of the Sunday he dubbed Victory Day because of the waves of "unspeakable glory" that swept over the service. Dr. Bresee rejected the idea of pledges; instead he raised cash by asking the people to march by the altar and lay their money on the Communion table. The altar was the sacred place where members and friends received the Lord's Supper, where couples were married, babies dedicated, and where the last remains of the saints were brought for a service before burial. The total ministry in Bresee's church focused on the sacred altar.

It is not possible to read Girvin's biography *A Prince in Israel* and not be struck by the great number of times the word *altar* shines forth from the pages like stars of the morning. Bresee was converted at an altar. He was sanctified at his own altar. He gathered funds for the permanent home of First Church at Sixth and Wall by receiving money at the altar. When the new building was dedicated, "before the dedicatory sermon could be preached, a man hurried to the altar" as 2,500 people watched and prayed. In Dr. Bresee's church the altar was the focus of everything that was vital and spiritually important. It was appropriate that he was buried from the altar of his own church.

When Dr. H. C. Morrison came to Los Angeles First Church for a revival, he said of the church, "The organization of this church grew out of strong opposition to the doctrine and experience of entire sanctification. The church was organized eight and a half years ago . . . and has grown to more than 1,600 members. I doubt if there is another congregation in the United States in a city with the population of Los Angeles, with so large a membership as this. . . . Thousands of souls have been converted or sanctified at the altars of this church . . . and go out to the ends of the earth to tell of the cleansing power of Christ's precious blood."

The fact is, there would be no Church of the Nazarene without the altar and the altar call. What Dr. Bresee was doing with the altar was similar to holiness evangelism in places like east Texas, Tennessee, New York, Rhode Island, and Illinois. It was the theology of the altar and the message of holiness that brought these people together in Pilot Point.

The question now is, what are we doing with the altar and where do we go from here? Every church has an altar, but how are we using it? How important is the altar to us today? And where are we headed tomorrow? These are some of the questions we will face in the three chapters of Division Four.

DIVISION FOUR

The Altar Today and Tomorrow

Oh! for the wonderful love He has promised,
  Promised for you and for me!
Though we have sinned, He has mercy and pardon,
  Pardon for you and for me.
        —from the hymn "Softly and Tenderly"

10

Focusing on Altar
Issues and Concerns

THERE ARE WAYS to help people relax, talk freely, and tell us what they really think. For instance, most people tend to relax while eating. We tend to talk more easily with people like ourselves, people with whom we have things in common. We usually open up best when we are not intimidated or pressured. And we talk more when the conversation is on topics that concern us. And always, we talk more easily and frankly in small groups than in large ones. The more personal the topic, the smaller the group. Some subjects will only be shared between two people; even a third person may increase the risk level enough to automatically shut off the conversation.

Examples of small groups that typically cover wide-ranging topics with few reservations include students in a dorm room on a campus, families enjoying a meal together, or colleagues gathered around the water cooler at work or sitting with their group at lunch.

Social scientists appropriated this concept of group talk, gave it a name, and developed the technique for gathering data on a given subject. These "focus groups," as they are called, usually consist of 6 to 12 people of divergent backgrounds who have one common cord that binds them together. They are brought together for a set time, asked to express themselves in the give-and-take of the situation, and are then dismissed and disbanded.

For instance, a car manufacturer may bring in a focus group consisting of people from varied professional backgrounds but with one common quality: They are yuppies. They are 25 to 40 years of age, married, without children, college educated, enjoying double incomes, and affluent. The manufacturer who brings in this kind of focus group expects to learn how yuppies feel about the automobiles they own and the car they would like to own. One focus group may render more good information than a dozen computers because people in focus groups can express feelings and sketch out thoughts beyond the scope of computers, which are programmed to deal only in digits. Focus groups may not be scientific, but they are certainly enlightening.

Excuse this long explanation, but the remainder of this chapter will have more meaning if we have some understanding of my techniques for learning where we are now in the use of the altar. I brought together six different kinds of focus groups to talk about the sacred altar. Although these groups came from varied backgrounds, they had a central characteristic that bound them together. The groups consisted of (1) denominational headquarters executives, (2) pastors, (3) Christian university faculty and administrators, (4) laymen, (5) district superintendents, and (6) full-time evangelists. With the exception of the evangelists each of these groups met at mealtime, listened to a brief summary from me on the first nine chapters on this book, and then responded with lively conversation on what they feel are the issues and concerns on the altar at this time. The evangelists had to be interviewed by phone because of the distance problems and conflicts in scheduling. Although each focus group had its own secretary to record their ideas, I made summary notes of my own. These observations are based on my own notes and the written report of each group secretary.

Summary Observations of Focus Group Sessions

1. Denominational Headquarters Executives

The first impression I gained from the headquarters group was their serious concern for the sacred altar and what they could do from headquarters to help maintain the altar in the central place of worship. Contrary to what some may think about the headquarters as a bureaucratic enclave, these men showed the same sensitivity and love for souls I later experienced with the pastors.

My second impression with the headquarters people was their resistance that bordered on antagonism against the open altar in Sunday morning worship. Some saw it as a substitute for the penitent altar, and certainly in competition with any invitation given at the end of the sermon. One leader said I could quote him: "I think the open altar is a deterrent to the altar call after the sermon." Another leader said, "I always ask the pastor to omit the open altar if he wants me to give an invitation after my sermon."

A third impression I received from the church executives was their ambivalence about altar abuse. This feeling took two directions: (1) Some were concerned about altar-call strategies that embarrassed people by separating them out in conspicuous ways, sometimes sending people away to return no more. (2) Others were concerned about adaptations of the traditional altar call that make people feel less conspicuous—sitting up straight to make direct eye contact with the preacher, lifting a hand for prayer without altar follow-through, and standing at the pew for prayer without going forward—as compromises on the traditional altar call.

Finally, I was impressed with the concern of the headquarters group about the options for educating and conditioning people on why the altar is important as a means of grace.

2. Pastors of Local Congregations

The pastors were protective of the open altar experience for their laymen on Sunday mornings. They believed that the altar call was important at the end of the sermon but that it failed to meet a basic spiritual need for people who also saw the altar as a means of grace for their problems in daily living. The different attitudes toward the open altar between head-quarters men and pastors may be the difference between men who live with their people week by week and con-nectional men who are invited in for a special service on evangelism, fund-raising, missionary emphasis, and the like.

Second, the pastors felt a need for planning the sermon, if not the entire service, to focus on the altar call. They talked about Billy Graham's strategy of mentioning the invitation before he begins his sermon and several times more while he preaches. This planning for the invitation is so much a part of Graham's way of doing things, the United Press International reported on his omission of the public invitation in China as though something important had been left out.

Again, pastors showed a concern for the shift in church architecture, which makes it harder to have a traditional altar service. Seats and pews have been installed closer together to get more seating per square foot of sanctuary. Space between the platform, Communion table, and altar are more cramped than they once were. The heavy cords and speaker devices installed for the benefit of people on the platform have com-plicated altar work and sometimes become a hazard to mov-ing about between the altar and the platform. Even the ugly installation of speakers, microphones, and other ampli-fication necessities have reduced the beauty and dignity of platforms that were once dominated by churchly simplicity.

Finally, pastors were supportive of the public altar but felt we should be open to other means of helping seekers, such as prayer rooms, adjustments in the procedures of the altar call, and wide and pervasive use of discipling materials that reinforce altar work. One pastor was visibly upset at a recent evangelist who, on the one hand, publicly suggested that the altar was for those feeling a need for a religious experience but who then urged the people to become like the early disciples who just turned from what they were doing and started following Jesus. Apparently the speaker who served as evangelist did not make a distinction between following Jesus as a vocation and turning to Him for forgiveness and cleansing from sin.

3. Christian University Faculty and Administration

I have been president of a Christian college or university for nearly 20 years, but I must confess my surprise at the depth of concern faculty members had for the sacred altar in all its spiritual ramifications. For starters, one Ph.D. in English was quick to express his concern for the children who are growing up in children's church and missing all the significance of the altar scene that impressed him deeply in his childhood years. This teacher is not a member of the generation about to retire. He is under 40, tools around in a BMW, and has a well-tuned sense of the fitness of things. Another faculty member spoke out in a scathing accusation that underscored his concern for children who have had little experience with the altar and the public invitation, in spite of child evangelism, Vacation Bible School, and other good programs. He startled us all when he blurted out, "Children's church is the worst thing that ever happened to us." We chided him good-naturedly for his overstatement, but everyone agreed that departmentalization has its downside. Everything in church programming is a trade-off. If we do one thing, we can't do another. And each choice in curriculum includes some things and excludes others. But I found that the faculty and administration were deeply concerned with the altar and the early spiritual experiences of the children.

This academic group had a thoughtful discussion on what they perceived as a shift in the theology of evangelism. We live in a culture that has extolled personal rights, privacy, and the equal value of all persons, while shifting to an intense resistance to appeals wrapped in emotion. Our adaptation to these cultural changes includes a strong promotion of friendship evangelism, a concern not to make people uncomfortable with a sermon that hammers away on ideas and words like repentance, contrition, restitution, hell, and judgment but focuses more on forgiveness, love, and acceptance. "Surely everybody is going to make it to heaven" is implied if not stated. Abstaining from sin has been transformed into a social responsibility for doing good to the less fortunate or refraining from behaviors with dire consequences that wind you up in an AIDS ward, drug or alcohol abuse rehabilitation center, or a divorce court. In our culture, people are not supposed to be put on the spot or made self-conscious, and no one is supposed to impose their value system on someone else, not even their children.

Faced with these cultural changes, the faculty and administration felt they saw a shift in our theology of evangelism. Pastors preach to be liked. Invitations are non-specific. There is more emphasis on a decision for Christ than on Christian experience. Following Christ is more of a pilgrimage than a relationship that begins in a crisis experience and is nurtured on obedience and a life separated from the world. The idea of spiritual struggle and release that evoked shouting in many places is a quaint memory to talk about in 75th anniversary services. Although these shifts in our theology of evangelism may be slight and sometimes imperceptible, they do change the way we look at the altar. As one faculty member put it, "There is no sense of defeat even if there are no seekers, week after week."

The faculty and administration spoke thoughtfully about the relationship of worship and evangelism. Should the morning and evening services be reflections of each other, or should there be distinct differences? Should not Sunday morning be the time for evangelism, since attendance at night is usually restricted to a smaller proportion of the church family unless there is a special program or a celebrity in concert? The morning service tends to be more formal and structured, while the invitation is by nature informal. Is there a way to blend these? Would it be better to close every service with a public invitation? A basketball player who wants to raise his point average per game is coached to make more shots. Does this analogy mean we need more invitations? Is the evening service the time to train and educate the families of the church in Christian concerns? Should Communion be shifted to Sunday evening when there is time for everyone to be served at the altar? What about the new direction in church scheduling being followed in an increasing number of new congregations who have services on Saturday evening and Sunday morning with no Sunday night service because it is a school night? All of these questions are provocative. There are no simple answers. But the church that is planning to make the altar central as a means of grace needs to explore these questions thoughtfully and prayerfully.

4. Laymen

With one exception, all of the laymen supported the idea of an open altar on Sunday morning and gave stories of their own personal help through this means of grace. Even the man who opposed the open altar idea in the opening moments of our discussion later agreed with the others on its importance, as long as it did not compete with the altar call following the sermon.

The greatest concern of the laymen was for the barren altars in their own local churches. One man who serves on a District Advisory Board said, "There have been times when we have gone 18 months without a seeker at the altar in our church." The others nodded. They tended to relate "dry altars," as they called them, to the style and concerns of the pastors. They said some pastors just don't know how to make an altar call. They said others seemed to be afraid of the people and almost apologized for the altar call. They loved the pastors who knew how to preach in a warmhearted way that made it easy for people to respond to their invitations.

Third, these laymen said that many in their congregations do not see the altar as a friendly place. As one layman put it, "Churches have a personality just like people; and our church has been a long time developing the altar as an unfriendly place."

Some laymen thought altar calls should be qualified so that people who wanted to pray alone could go to one end of the altar, and those who wanted the comfort and counsel of others praying with them would kneel at the other end. I wondered if this might not further complicate the altar call, but they didn't think so.

The most insistent concern of the laymen was on the importance of the altar. One layman said they bought a building from the Christian Reformed church, which had no altar. "We chose one of the pews for the altar lumber, and we made our own altar. It was beautiful. And we made it. I will never forget the first man who knelt at our altar. I still remember his name although that was years ago, and he has long since gone on to heaven. But he was saved at the altar we made with our own hands." Another told about the instructions to their architect when a new sanctuary was being planned. "We wanted our same pulpit and altar transferred from the old building to the new one. The architect didn't like the idea, but we did it anyhow. The builders refinished the altar and made it look like new. But it was still our old altar, and we loved keeping it." There is much to be said for continuity.

One layman from a thriving little church in a small county town said, "I didn't know there was any problem with the altar until I came here today. We have just believed the altar is for helping people, and that is how we have used ours."

Before the laymen left my table, I summarized their concerns and then asked if my summary was correct. The laymen I talked with were concerned about (1) preserving the best there is in the open altar idea. (2) They feel a need for more specific altar calls, made more often, in ways that will be honored by the Holy Spirit, and therefore result in people coming forward. (3) Laymen believe Communion is important and were open to the idea of a Communion service at night with the elements served at the altar by the pastor. (4) All of the laymen feel a need for more churchwide education about the altar and how it can be used as a means of grace.

5. District Superintendents

Nine of the 11 district superintendents I invited to this focus group were present in spite of their schedules, which are subject to many last-minute conflicts. Their responses made me know that these church leaders are deeply concerned about the altar and its continuing use in the church.

I was especially impressed with their discussion on the sacredness of the altar. One superintendent said, "I see the altar used for stacking books, displaying flowers, standing, sitting and visiting, being encumbered with sound equipment, and nearly any other utilitarian use you can imagine. They even let the children play on it." Others suggested the Communion table was often used for flower displays and not for the symbols of our faith.

This discussion on the sacredness of the altar was followed by another discussion of all of the uses for the altar besides the public invitation. These include (1) dedications, (2) baptisms, (3) ordinations, (4) healing services, (5) installation services, (6) Communion, (7) church membership, (8) sending services, and even (9) march offerings.

These district superintendents were concerned about the discipling of new Christians after an altar experience. One of them said, "I would encourage you to write a second book, *Beyond the Altar,* dealing with how to live the Christian life after the altar experience."

They also saw an issue in the reluctance of laymen in the churches and even pastors at camp meeting services to come forward with seekers for prayer. In some churches the congregation is dismissed before the prayers around the altar begin.

The superintendents were concerned with most of the

issues the other focus groups discussed. However, they had an additional concern for pastors as models for young preachers in giving a good invitation, creating the atmosphere that makes it easy for people to move forward and to enjoy a victorious altar experience. They see this need for good models starting with pastors in the local church, where most young men and women are called into full-time Christian service, and continuing through college and seminary with classroom instruction, hands-on experience. They believed it is especially important to provide Spirit-anointed models for students to observe during the years of formal education for the ministry.

6. Full-time Evangelists

My contacts with the full-time evangelists were by necessity on the phone, individually. I called at the beginning of the week when most of them were home following the closing of revivals the previous Sunday night. Their diversions on their day off were interesting to me. One came to talk with me from the garden where he was weeding the flowers. Another crawled out from beneath a car where he was working. He said fixing cars cleared out his mind. One was home after several weeks on the road and looking forward to fixing his boat. Another was just home from commencement in a Christian college that had given him an honorary degree. He was very happy about what the recognition meant for evangelists in general. It struck me again that these men are just regular people who also have a significant life off the platform. They are God-called men, but they are men, good men. They spoke to me easily and without apology. They were straightforward about their issues and concerns for the altar.

Without exception, these men were much less concerned with the invitation than they were with the lack of altar workers. At the top of their agendas was their concern for quality in altar work. One of these men called his first concern, "Shallow work at the altar." The altar is not a means of grace in itself. It takes more than touching the altar to appropriate its benefits. As one evangelist put it, "There is no grace in the wood."

One evangelist with a national and international ministry said he was concerned about the decline in the intensity of prayer, the lack of involvement of Christians in the pews, and the frightening lack of workers who show genuine feeling for the seekers. We now specialize in shorter, less involved prayers. "The altar sounds like a morgue, not a maternity ward."

Many seekers come to the altar from a state of rebellion. They need time to pray alone. Then they need counsel that helps them keep to the issue. The wrong kind of counselors at the altar can get the seeker off his own needs to the concerns of the altar worker.

None of these evangelists mentioned the use of the Bible in altar work. This by no means indicates they do not believe in using the Bible to help seekers. But I do believe it means these evangelists are concerned that seekers "pray through," or "find victory," or "come to a new knowledge of Christ Jesus." Scripture with faith is the basis for certitude and growth. As one evangelist put it, "We don't just walk them through when they come to the altar; we pray them through."

Besides their concern for good altar work, these evangelists were equally concerned about the use of the open altar, which seems to "water down more specific invitations." There are no testimonies following the open altar, no declarations of triumph, just relief and assurance. Time seems to be the great enemy. The open altar can be controlled and limited; but in an altar service that lengthens out, there is sensitivity about the volunteer nursery workers and the children in children's churches, and just the concern of the people for what they plan to do after the service is over.

Another evangelist said the open altar "takes the edge off the altar call." Anyone who comes forward in the open altar will not likely come again during the altar call after the sermon. Therefore, the open altar becomes one more obstacle in trying to get people saved and sanctified. "You can't have it both ways." All of the evangelists agreed the open altar should be omitted during revival time, "otherwise people are likely to leave with their deeper spiritual needs unmet."

A third concern that was shared by all the evangelists was the need to restore a spirit of anticipation, expectation, and excitement to the altar call and the altar service. One evangelist deals with this concern by postponing his invitation to the final Sunday morning so that the people can think about the messages and their own spiritual needs. This waiting, according to him, makes the people more ready for a deeper spiritual work when they do go forward. The evangelists seemed to feel frustration in trying to do a deep, lasting work with spiritual quality when the mood of the day and sometimes the attitude of the church works against them. The total altar experience needs to be genuine spiritual therapy. "The altar is the most spiritually therapeutic place in the world."

Three of the nine evangelists with whom I talked were concerned about the possible tendency toward idolatry of the wooden bench we call the altar. "Numbers are not important. People are!" In some places people have become conditioned to the availability of grace only after a vigorous sermon usually in the evening or on Sunday mornings just before dinner. One evangelist even suggested we may be on the verge of a whole new way of dealing with the spiritual needs of people that puts the altar in an entirely new perspective. His startling suggestion reminded me of the closing words of Dr. Robert E. Coleman in his study, *The Origin of the Altar Call in American Methodism:* "Perhaps a new and even more indigenous invitation will emerge. But, like it or not, until there can be found an evangelistic method more suited to the temperament and aspirations of the American people, the 'altar call' of the distinctively revivalist origin and flavor is likely to remain a vital part of evangelical worship."

Summary of Issues and Concerns

With information I have gleaned from talking with six different groups—denominational executives, pastors, Christian faculty and administration, laymen, district superintendents, and full-time evangelists—the following are their combined issues and concerns.

1. Are we desecrating or neglecting the sacredness of the altar? Is the importance of the altar losing ground to new methods and new ways of thinking?

2. What attitude should we take toward the open altar? Does the open altar compete with the altar call? Can they be harmonized?

3. Does the trend toward nonspecific altar calls dilute the evangelistic thrust for sinners to be saved and believers to be sanctified? Why do people go forward and kneel at the altar?

4. Has the altar call been abused? Is there a stigma that won't go away?

5. What architectural problems need to be faced in building sanctuaries for evangelism?

6. How can pastors learn to give effective altar invitations? Where are the teachers who can show the way by example? And how can young ministers be brought to know them?

7. Has the time come for educating or reeducating the people about the purposes of the altar? Do we have a generation of children and teens who are unfamiliar with the altar?

8. Has there been a shift in our theology of evangelism? Are we more concerned these days with process than crisis?

9. What can pastors and congregations do about consistently barren altars? How can a spiritually dead church be rekindled?

10. Does it matter that Communion is usually served in the seats, or should new means be developed for serving Communion at the altar?

11. What can be done to conserve the fruit of the altar? In too many places, congregations are faced with a revolving-door evangelism that fails to assimilate the new converts into the life of the church.

This concludes my report on how the issues and concerns about the altar were identified and what these issues are. We turn next to the task of reporting on how these issues are faced in the churches with more than 200 members that are growing the most, and in the churches over 200 members that are slow growing or not growing at all. At this point in the preparation I didn't know how this study would turn out. I hadn't even begun to collect the data from these pastors. So I let it lead where it would. It was better that way.

11

The Altar in Fast-Growing Churches

A FTER using the focus groups to identify the issues and concerns about the altar, the next step in this phase of the study was to identify the fast-growing churches and the slow-growing churches to determine what differences, if any, there were in their attitudes toward the altar and the way it is used in their services. Some of the fast-growing churches had taken in more than 100 new members during the last year, while some of the slower-growing churches, each with more than 200 members, had not taken in any new members during the year in study and were demonstrating a struggle to grow, as revealed by the computer numbers covering a four-year span.

Before starting to talk with these men, I decided to let the truth lead wherever it would. I really thought the pastors of slower-growing churches would report extenuating circumstances beyond their control, thus getting themselves off the hook for slow growth. But this was not the case.

I also thought some of the faster-growing churches might have new feelings about the altar as a means of grace.

Perhaps they had forsaken the altar for other methods. But this was not the case either.

The conclusion was that pastors in both fast-growing churches and slow-growing churches were very much alike. They are good men, sincere, faithful to the church, and concerned about their people. However, as conversations with pastors in fast-growing churches and those in slow-growing churches continued, I began to feel and then to identify some differences I believe are significant. These are not differences of character, commitment, or even hard work; but there are differences. After a great many conversations with pastors in both fast- and slow-growing churches, I began to anticipate their responses because they followed a pattern.

1. *Pastors in fast-growing churches seemed to focus on solutions instead of problems.*

For instance, almost all pastors talked about the letdown in interest among Christian people for doing altar work. However, pastors in slow-growing churches felt victimized, while pastors in fast-growing churches responded immediately with what they were doing to recruit and train adequate altar workers.

2. *Pastors in slow-growing churches had very little altar anticipation.*

These pastors were afraid of failure. They did not expect much response from the congregation to the open altar, and especially to the altar call at the end of the sermon. These pastors talked about the need for more prayer in their congregations, but none of them attached the idea to results at the altar. Since they believe prayer is needed, they urge people to pray; but it is a function, an end in itself, and not part of their concept of the altar as a means of grace. These pastors are in a "down" mood about the open altar and the altar call. In these churches the open altar attracts "the same people each week," and they feel there is a stigma about the altar. As proof, one pastor cited his statistics: "We have only had four seekers this year."

3. *Without exception, pastors in fast-growing churches were able to articulate their concept of the altar and evangelism.*

Conceptual thinking is the ability to see the whole picture at once and know what to do about any part of it, down to the smallest detail. The president of Sears came into my office once and said he would pay me the largest fee Sears had ever paid if I could tell him how to teach conceptual thinking to Sears managers. If this kind of thinking is important to Sears, it is all the more important to the pastor who visualizes the altar as a primary means of grace.

Any pastor can go through the functions of the altar call, just because he knows how. But pastors in fast-growing churches have a mental picture of the entire altar service. One pastor told me he could tell in advance who was coming to the altar by looking at their faces. Another told me he literally saw Jesus standing at the altar, hands outstretched. He saw himself as the proclaimer, not sharing Christ but calling the people to Christ, who is the Divine Altar. A pastor in a slow-growing church said it was discouraging to give an invitation and fail one more time. "Nobody comes to the altar anymore."

4. *The pastors in the fast-growing churches were enthusiastic about their outreach programs.*

These pastors saw new people as their primary source for the altar call and church membership. One pastor told me about the ministry in his parking lot where a man who is widely known, but loyal to his parking lot ministry, greets drivers and shows them where to park. In January, when the temperature was in the teens and the loose snow was blowing to and fro, a car pulled into the parking lot because the driver intended to turn around. Since the lot is parked solid to conserve space for a fast-growing congregation, the greeter just directed the driver into a row of cars, and in seconds another auto was behind it, locking him in. It would have been hard now for him to turn around and leave. When the driver saw he was caught, he asked, "What kind of church is this?"

"Nazarene!" the parking lot greeter answered with enthusiasm, in spite of the shivering weather and upturned flaps on his storm coat.

"Is it like a Baptist church?"

"Somewhat!"

"Is it like a Methodist church?"

"Somewhat! You just come on in. You'll like our people, and you'll hear a good sermon."

The stranger and his wife entered the sanctuary, choosing cautiously to sit on the back row. They had never known anything about Nazarenes. However, they were reassured by examining the hymnbook, which was filled with familiar hymns. The music was inspiring. The people sang heartily, and the choir performed well. The sermon was helpful. After the service the people who greeted them were open and friendly. The entire worship experience was positive.

The next Sunday the couple who were caught in the parking lot by accident the previous week came back to church on purpose. Within three months they were assimilated into the congregation. They finished the pastor's membership class. And they started tithing. Their tithe is equal to the weekly salary of one of the associate pastors. The pastor who told me this story is enthusiastic about his church and his outreach program to new people. His enthusiasm is typical of pastors in faster-growing churches. I'm sure he is not the only pastor whose parking lot is an important factor in evangelism.

5. *Pastors of fast-growing churches have made the altar a friendly place.*

Fast-growing churches have found ways to eliminate any stigma in going to the altar, while "stigma" was often mentioned as a negative factor by pastors in slow-growing churches. It's a basic difference in attitude. As mentioned earlier, one black pastor of a thriving church that is close to doubling its size in the last four years put it best of all: "In our church, the altar is a sign of our trust in God, not a sign of our failure."

The basic difference between the way the altar is used in the faster-growing churches and the slower-growing churches is an attitude, a way of thinking about the altar. Some churches see the altar as a place of last desperation, while others see it as a convenient place to talk with God, in His house, surrounded by His people. When Mary and Joseph lost Jesus for three days in Jerusalem, they looked for Him in the Temple as a last act of desperation after three fruitless days in a wandering search. There were probably people who saw them headed into the Temple and said to each other, "I wonder what they've done wrong."

On the Resurrection side of the Cross, Christ is the Altar. The wooden bench where people kneel to pray may be plain or elaborate. It does not really matter. Since the altar is a convenient place to meet Christ, how can it be anything but friendly! Christ said, "Come unto me all ye that labour and are heavy laden, and I will give you rest" (Matt. 11:28). What a shame for the altar in any church to be an unfriendly place.

Attitudes Toward the Altar in Faster-Growing Churches

Sacredness of the Altar

The first pastor I interviewed summarized in one succinct statement what I was to hear from the other pastors of growing churches: "We don't spend a lot of time deifying the altar. It is sacred when we use it for spiritual purposes, and the rest of the time it is a piece of church furniture that can even be moved in and out of the sanctuary according to our needs."

This idea of "sacred use" instead of "sacred furniture" was dominant among these pastors because they are action-oriented men, highly focused on results and not given to much symbolism. Another study has shown that they also do not use the ecclesiastical shorthand of cherished words in their preaching but use the concepts of sacred words with adequate explanations and illustrations. Slow-growing churches are atuned to sounds and feelings, while fast-growing churches combine something to think about with something to feel and something to do.

The pastor of a church with a well-established pattern of growth said, "I think things, by their very nature, should be utilitarian. They are just there for sacred use. The altar is a functional piece of furniture, a convenient place to pray. The altar is not only a place to symbolize God but also a place to keep in touch. Christ is the Altar, not the kneeling bench where we pray."

The pastor of one of the largest churches in this study echoed the same idea: "The altar is sacred only because of what happens there." But he went on to relate another dimension of sacredness to the altar. "It is what happens there that keeps our people in awe and wonder of the altar." If "awe and wonder" can be synonymous with "sacred use of the altar," then many of us would agree with the pastor who said to me, over and over, "The altar is the foundation and strength of our church." This is why another pastor saw sacredness in the testimonies made concerning altar experiences, even identifying an exact spot where a person was saved or sanctified, or where some great burden was lifted, or a spiritual battle won.

All of these pastors were sensitive to the sacredness of the altar, even to honoring its place in the trinity of sacred furniture, along with the pulpit and the Communion table. One man said, "I don't like to see children climbing over it, but it doesn't help that we are in a multipurpose auditorium. The altar of itself doesn't look sacred. And, besides that, it's just the right height for kids."

In summary, pastors of faster-growing churches are not hung up over the sacredness of the altar as a piece of church furniture, but they have strong feelings about the sacredness of what happens there.

A Variety of Ideas
Concerning the Open Altar

Pastors of the faster-growing churches all appreciate the open altar, but they do not think alike concerning its use. Here are some typical responses:

"During the morning services I feel led about half the time to have an open altar, but never when I plan to give an invitation at the end of my sermon. . . . About half of the people who come are the same ones each time. . . . Where people sit has something to do with whether or not they come forward to the open altar. The farther back they sit, the less likely they are to come. And no one comes from the balcony."

Another pastor said, "I am very positive about the open altar. I use it every week on Wednesday nights. The open altar on Sunday mornings competes with the regular altar call. . . . Yes, I give an altar call about half the time on Sunday mornings, depending on the theme of my sermon."

Another pastor of an equally large and growing church said, "The open altar does not compete with the regular altar call. But it should be structured so that people tend to come for like purposes. I have an open altar about half the time, but I give an altar call almost every Sunday."

Another pastor, who was at the top of the list of new members received in the year of this study, said, "The altar is a place of many purposes. The family altar should be as open and wide as the needs of the people. . . . I don't give an altar call every Sunday for two reasons. First, it tends to upset the arrangements that are necessary for multiple services. One week I went overtime 10 minutes in the altar call, and it caused utter havoc in the parking lot, to say nothing about the problems it created in the changing of Sunday School classes, nursery problems, and children's church. When I use the open altar, I can regulate the length of my sermon, but it is hard to regulate the time people will use to pray in the altar call. And second, we have not worked out the problem of adequate altar workers. It may be heresy, but I think we would do better to take people into a prayer room after the altar call, give them adequate spiritual help and sufficient time to pray, and get out from under the gun of the clock."

But another pastor with multiple services did not see any problem with the altar call at the end of the sermon. "We just plan for it and omit the open altar on the Sundays I expect to give an invitation. Furthermore, it doesn't hurt people to come into an auditorium for the next service while people from the last one are still praying."

One pastor whose loyalty and doctrinal commitments could never be questioned reported to me on a whole new approach that replaces the traditional open altar. "I think the open altar has been overworked and overused. The open altar keeps some people from being chronic seekers, but they have less victory at the open altar than they used to get during the altar service when they were surrounded by a spiritual support group. . . . I grow tired of the same group coming forward each week in the open altar. And I'm sure it took away from the altar call. . . . I decided to divide the congregation into prayer circles of four or five people, right where they are sitting in the pews. The devil told me people wouldn't like it and the plan wouldn't work. But I wanted to see everybody talking to each other and praying for each other. I finally got up my nerve to try the small prayer groups. And now our people just love it. Everybody has something to be grateful for and something to be concerned about. No one is put on the spot, but everyone is asked to express his gratitude and concern, then the person on his left prays for him. If someone doesn't want to pray aloud, we just ask the next person to pray, and move on. It sounds like the praying used to sound in our churches when everyone prayed at once. And really that is what we are doing. About a fourth of the congregation is praying at any one time. This lasts about five minutes, and then I pray the pastoral prayer. It takes a little time, but we love the procedure because everyone gets involved. And furthermore, this approach helps the altar call and does not compete with it."

Specific or Nonspecific Invitations

All of the pastors in the faster-growing churches agreed on the need to combine the specific and the nonspecific invitations. It was said best by a pastor with wide experience, "I am nonspecific because the people come on their own terms anyhow. I used to be very explicit about coming to be saved, to be sanctified, or to be reclaimed. Then when I got down to pray with a seeker, they were likely to tell me they were praying for a relative or for their physical healing."

One effective pastor-evangelist said he always starts off with a general invitation and then becomes more specific. "People coming begets more people coming. And sometimes I find that people who come under a general invitation are counseled and realize their specific need to be saved or sanctified."

One pastor said he divided the altar. Those who have personal problems kneel at one end, and those with specific spiritual needs to be saved or sanctified kneel at the other.

One very thoughtful response came from a pastor who said, "I think we fail to appreciate the stamp the camp meeting movement has made on us in our focus on the altar call. Camp meeting preaching in the old days was directed entirely toward an altar response and very little on the problems of living the Christian life. If a pastor stays long enough and preaches comprehensively, people will know where they are spiritually, with or without the altar. I believe we should focus on preaching and let the altar response be directed by the Holy Spirit."

Manipulations and Abuses in the System of Altar Calls

The main problem with manipulation and abuses is the problem of long memories. As one pastor explained, "There are just some evangelists our people won't have back. And this is hard because these evangelists are my friends. Our congregation has a long memory. They won't tolerate abuses.

They want integrity. They want to be dealt with honestly and openly."

As another pastor said, "Our people seem to have long memories. They have a mental block because of past experiences. And many of these people who resist the altar are our local church leaders. They don't come forward for the open altar, or for that matter, to pray with seekers during the altar service. But with the new people, and the young people, there are no hang-ups."

The pastor of a very large church closed our interview with this word: "When my uncle was a young man, he used to talk about how wonderful it would be to have all of the evangelists' stories in a book. Then he went into the ministry. And after five or six years as pastor, he told me one day that there was no need for the book because those stories were in his congregation every Sunday. I guess people don't need to be manipulated or abused; they just need help."

Architecture and the Altar

All of these pastors in growing churches are concerned about architects who did not plan for evangelism. To increase seating, pews have often been too close together for people to kneel easily. The pulpit, Communion table, and altar do not always harmonize as one significant center of spiritual concern. Choirs are usually better lighted than Communion tables and altars. The crowded relationship of the Communion table to the pulpit and altar often obstruct easy passage of altar workers. Even the sound monitors, cables, and other high-tech gear fight against sacredness and sometimes create hazards.

One pastor said, "Harmony and beauty in the church furniture is often an afterthought. In our church, the organ and piano are twice as prominent as the pulpit, Communion table, and altar. It bothers me every week."

Another said, "I wish we had kneeling benches or at least soft carpet so that the people can kneel forward. I tried it once, and it was terrific. We closed our prayer time that Sunday morning by singing 'The Lord's Prayer.'"

Another frustrated man, referring to the high-tech equipment, said, "Let's get rid of the junk! And we intend to in our new building."

Another pastor who already enjoys a new building, including the debt, said with great joy, "We researched all of that before we built. The altar is a good height for kneeling. It's wide enough for a Bible to be laid on it. There is a shelf on the back side for anointing oil, tissue, and other needs. It took courage, but we paid the price in square feet to have ample space on both sides of the altar and around the Communion table. We even have room for the orchestra on the platform without cluttering the space around the altar."

In contrast, another pastor suffering growing pains said, "We have paid a price to increase seating. The configuration around our altar is not good, but we just go on and do our job anyhow. Someday we'll do better, but we can't wait for then."

Learning to Give an Effective Altar Call

Two of the most successful pastor-evangelists I talked with suggested, partly in jest, that their ability to give an effective invitation was inherited. However, each of them went on to acknowledge they learned how to give an effective invitation by watching their fathers and grandfathers. The ability to give an effective invitation is learned by observing someone who is a good model. Some pastors readily named the persons they watched and learned from. However, one analytical pastor believed we should combine classroom study, campus visits by good resource people, and effective pastors in college, university, and seminary centers as the combined means for teaching young people to be effective in giving an invitation.

Education of the People
Concerning the Meaning of the Altar

Although this issue was a matter of concern among the focus groups, especially the laymen, the pastors of these fastest-growing churches did not seem to be much concerned and did not have special programs for education on the altar. They all felt they took care of this matter in their preaching. "Everyone Jesus called, He called publicly." If this is the New Testament norm, then we only need to make the altar a friendly place where the call to follow Him can be made.

All of these growing churches have pastor's classes, membership classes, and catechism classes for the children. But none of these pastors depend on these classes for educating the people on the purposes and importance of the altar. This is done from the pulpit.

Is There a Shift in Our Theology of Evangelism?

In the early days of Francis Asbury's Methodism in America, seekers came to the mourner's bench, where they fought a battle with their evil nature. Finally, after a struggle, seekers broke through to victory in a burst of emotion that made shouting a natural response. Subsequent songs, testimonies, and sermons about this victory often rekindled memories and feelings that resulted in more shouting. In time shouting became a conditioned response to a warm-hearted service. This open demonstration of heavenly joy became a much-anticipated part of worship. I have heard many stories about my grandmother shouting all the way home from church, unconcerned that neighbors along the country road were listening and watching. But the grandmothers of my children never shouted, although they were fine examples of Christian faith.

There has been a shift in our attention, if not in our expectations, of grace as a means to salvation. We hear very little about the struggle at the altar. Altar prayers are shorter. Struggling against evil has given way to acceptance and saying, "Yes!" We seem to be much more concerned with the process of Christian living than the critical nature of Christian experience. We focus more on the problems of following the Way than on entering it.

None of the pastors in these growing churches rejected the idea that we have had a shift in our theology of evangelism, which is not to be confused with our systematic theology. We continue to interpret the Bible as Wesleyan-Arminian theologians who have made ample room for man's responsibility and free will. We believe in the Triune God. We believe the Bible as the revealed Word of God, that God created the world and crowned His creation with Adam and Eve. We believe man is lost and can be restored to a right relationship with God and his fellowman through forgiveness of sins and the cleansing of the sin nature through Jesus Christ. Because man is still human, and is never faultless in mind or behavior, sin is a willful transgression of a known law. And finally, we believe in eternal rewards and punishment in heaven or hell.

However, there are three tension points in our theology of evangelism: (1) The stress between crisis and process. (2) What we do really believe about heaven and hell. (3) The stress between cognitive mental assent for salvation, as practiced in much of evangelical Calvinism, and personal experience with Christ, as known in Wesleyan evangelism in America's early days.

First, either we have shifted away from crisis, or we have included the spiritual process more fully than before. Several of the pastors I talked with felt we have shifted away from crisis in favor of process, that "we have overreacted," or "the pendulum effect has taken over," or what is happening these days in our preaching and in our altar calls is in reaction "to the overselling of the crisis experience as a spiritual cure-all." One pastor asked, "Does the Bible say, 'Go and make' disciples, or does it say, 'Go make' disciples?" Another one said, "We have a healthier understanding of crisis and process." They all said, "We need both."

In all our theology books, we make strong statements on eternal rewards and punishment. But in sermons, church programming, and expressions of personal concern as repeated in prayers and conversations, we are not afraid of hell as we once were. Some people have the idea that God is too good to allow anyone to be lost. Maybe this feeling is a matter of the pendulum effect that time will correct.

And third, are we more Calvinistic than we once were in our approaches to evangelism? Certainly our children in Bible clubs at school and in most para-church organizations are fully exposed to a Calvinistic approach to salvation. One president of a renowned holiness college told me that the magazines he sees most often on the coffee tables in the homes of his alumni are produced on good Calvinist presses. In fact, how many holiness magazines do you know that are published for Christian families? Dr. Kennedy's personal evangelism program is based on accepting certain truths from the Scripture, and "Happy Birthday!" you've been born anew. His program, along with the idea of the four spiritual laws, is a cognitive approach through mental assent and not a sharp focus on personal experience. We have always had an emotional, experience-centered approach to salvation, but in many places there is a shift under way to a cognitive approach based on biblical understanding and mental assent.

The answer to all of these shifts in our theology of evangelism is a matter of balance. All of the pastors seemed to feel this need for balance. "We need to preach on how to win the game, but first we need to get our man on first, then we'll coach him on to second." We need the Bible principles for personal evangelism for altar work, but not to the exclusion of the concern for personal experience. No one can oppose the need for crisis and process. You can't have one without the other.

Consistently Barren Altars

None of the pastors of growing churches complained about barren altars. One pastor said it for all of them: "We enjoy a good stream of people who seek the Lord." Another pastor pinpointed the reason for barren altars: "It comes from a lack of successful outreach programs."

Communion at the Altar

All of these pastors of growing churches serve Communion on Sunday mornings in the pews. As they all said, "It's a matter of available time, although the altar is really the place to celebrate Communion." However, each of these pastors serves Communion at the altar by families, once or twice a year, usually at Christmas or New Year's Eve. As one pastor said, "This amounts to a series of 15-minute services, by appointment." Also several of these pastors from faster-growing churches reported good attendance for a Communion service once or twice monthly at 8:30 A.M. on Sunday.

Beyond the Altar Is There Follow-through?

Each of these pastors in fast-growing churches has a follow-up program for all new converts. It begins with a phone call or visit by a designated person. And it continues with Bible study groups and pastor's classes. As one said, "We do everything to conserve the fruit of our altar. We work too hard to win them to lose them over spiritual and personal neglect."

Unstructured Pastoral Responses

At the end of my interview with each pastor, I asked if they had anything additional to say on anything relating to the altar. Was there anything that he felt keenly about that was not covered in the structured interview? Here is a sample of the responses:

"Unless the Church of the Nazarene holds the line on preaching evangelistically for decisions, we won't need any altar."

"I am glad we have an altar. I work in a variety of ways to enhance the use of the altar in weddings, baby dedications, baptisms, sending services, and installations. I urge our people to plan their funeral services in the church. Wesley said, 'Our people die well.' It is the privilege of every believer to be buried from the altar of the church."

"I am very comfortable right where we are."

"The key idea with me on altar services is the word *breakthrough*. If there are not enough spiritual breakthroughs in the church, it's because there are not enough altar services with good altar experiences."

12 ≡

The Altar in Slow-Growing Churches

AFTER TALKING with a significant number of pastors in churches that are not growing, I was puzzled. Their lack of growth is an enigma. The reasons seem hidden and uncertain. Among pastors there is no dividing line in years of formal education between those whose churches grow and those that don't. The difference is not between orthodoxy and unorthodoxy, or in degrees of concern for the holiness ethic. I reluctantly conclude again for the second time in this study that the basic difference between faster- and slower-growing churches is in attitude and concept, not functions. Pastors in churches on dead center are good men doing the right things, but all the good things they do just don't result in success. There is always something missing in the picture.

We need to pray for these pastors with churches that don't grow. The problem is not with the spiritual and moral quality of these men. They are fine pastors. And their congregations consist of fine people. Some fail the attitude test because they are not happy and enthusiastic about the altar and all the work it represents. Or they fail to have a strategic plan for winning new families. Or both! Neither of these failures is irreversible. A pastor can learn to be happy and enthusiastic. And a pastor can learn to develop a strategic plan for winning souls.

The Sacredness of the Public Altar

There is a strong commitment to the sacredness of the altar, as the altar, among these pastors. For most of these men the altar is sacred when it is used for sacred purposes and when it is not. But most of them have had an attitudinal hang-up of some kind concerning the use of the altar.

One man who has been a pastor for more than 25 years said, "The altar is not as sacred as it once was. I don't know why. People are not committed to the use of the altar as they once were. Counseling is where I lead people to the Lord, and not at the altar."

Another pastor with much the same feelings said, "There is a stigma attached to the altar, an aversion to it. The 30-year members, who have certainly been around long enough to know better, will not even come down to pray with people. . . . There is great respect for the altar as church furniture. Our people have high regard for the altar, but they are not responsive to invitations. Maybe a dozen times in my five years."

One Midwest pastor said, "Our people see the altar as very sacred. They don't allow children to play on it, and no adults sit on it. We are preserving the altar, not using it."

The Open Altar and the Altar Call

"We use the open altar every Sunday," one pastor said with a sense of commitment in his voice. Then he went on to say, "But I had to line up the board members to use the open altar and set the example for the others. . . . We have an altar call nearly every Sunday morning, but unfortunately, we have had less than a half dozen seekers so far this year." He said his assembly year was about two-thirds gone.

A pastor said, "We have an open altar every Sunday morning. It is well received because of their resistance to the altar call. But I must say, it's the same 12 to 15 people each week. Not much victory."

Another pastor in a nonthriving church in a thriving city said, "The same people come to the open altar. They use it twice a month. . . . I've wondered if it does compete with my altar call."

One pastor who is particularly enthusiastic about the open altar said, "We use it every Sunday morning and sometimes on Sunday night. . . . They come according to felt need, so many in the church participate over a period of time. . . . It does affect the altar call because some have been saved at the open altar. I consider it as a part of my altar call." I believe he would agree with another pastor who said, "The open altar does compete with the altar call, and that's all right with me."

Nonspecific and Specific Invitations

I received a series of gloomy responses from these men concerning the issue of the specific and the nonspecific invitation. One man said, "Our people don't even come forward for the nonspecific invitations." I preached in one of these churches where the pastor told me there had not been a seeker in a year. To my joy and his, three people came forward. But he was right: No one came forward to pray with them.

Another discouraged pastor just replied, "I have no thoughts on the subject."

Several men responded to the issue of nonspecific invitations versus specific invitations by bringing his evangelists into the picture: "I try to be specific but not with much success, one or two a month on the average. But our evangelists don't do much better. . . . I'm disappointed in evangelists who don't get down to business until Sunday. They just use general invitations weeknights."

Another said, "I open the altar with a nonspecific invitation about twice a month, but the response is sporadic and sparse. The evangelists give specific invitations, but their response is slow, too."

One pastor who felt especially defeated on altar calls and revivals said, "Evangelists and revivals in our church are just not a success. They give a general invitation toward the end so that we can feel we had a good meeting. . . . My invitation is always tied to the theme of the sermon, but I don't have very good results either."

Altar Call Manipulations and Abuses

Since several of the pastors in fast-growing churches were concerned about the integrity of the altar call and the need to be sure there were no abuses or manipulations, it was interesting that pastors in the slow-growing churches were unanimous in reporting "no problems." One pastor said he had heard about people who hadn't been back to the church because they were offended at revival techniques 10 and 15 years ago, but there certainly were no concerns now.

One pastor in a western mountain city said, "There could have been problems except that our people are wonderful, warmhearted people, and they just let things like that go. . . . No problems with us." The remainder of the responses to the idea of abuses included "No. . . . We don't have numbers, anyhow. . . . Has not happened here. . . . Every evangelist knows we don't look at numbers, so, no abuses."

The Church Altar
and Architectural Problems

There was little or no concern among pastors of slow-growing churches concerning ample space to work around the altar or to kneel between the pews. Apparently there are other more important problems much higher on their agendas.

Effective Altar Calls

Only one pastor in the entire group had any self-doubt concerning his own ability to give an effective invitation. He said, "I wish I were better. I'm so afraid of being a manipulator that I don't push very hard." Others said, "Growing up in church made giving an altar call come second nature." Another said, "I learned a lot from watching special speakers." Still another, "No problem. They even had altar calls on Wednesday night in the church where I grew up." Another good man I know very well said, "I don't have any trouble making an altar call, but I also don't get very good responses." Maybe the best answer came from the pastor who said, "I don't know what makes an effective altar call. It's not so much a matter of skill. . . . Maybe it just depends on the Holy Spirit."

Education of the People

The pastors of the slow-growing churches showed good insights when asked about the issue of educating the people on the meaning and purpose of the altar. One man said, "We're trying. But it is mostly a matter of reeducation in our church, and that is tougher."

One man blurted out, "It's not a matter of education. Our people already understand about the purpose of the altar; it's a matter of getting them to do something about it." Still another one said flatly, "We're not doing anything to educate our people, but it sounds like a good idea."

One frustrated pastor said, "I don't have any programs for teaching people about the altar. But I preach on it every year, sometimes twice. . . . It took me a year before anyone responded to the open altar. . . . In our church there is just a stigma about going to the altar. . . . They think going to the altar means somebody has had a moral breakdown."

Shift in Our Theology of Evangelism

The pastors of these slow-growing churches used their strongest rhetoric on their perceptions of a shift in our theology of evangelism from crisis to process, and from experience to daily grace for daily living. For starters one man said, "We have discipled ourselves out of evangelism." I should have asked him what he meant by that, but his strong statement startled me, and I moved on to another question.

One pastor said, "I recognize the shift. I think it took place in the 1950s and 1960s. . . . But I think there is a new shift going on now, back to crisis theology." Another pastor said he believed there had been a definite shift away from crisis experience to pilgrimage and discipling. "But it hasn't happened in my church."

One thoughtful pastor suggested a partial reason for the shift: "We are a lot more sophisticated in our reading nowadays. And Ogilvie and Swindoll don't have altars in their churches, and they don't write about being saved and sanctified, either. We have walked away from fire and brimstone talk, just like they have."

Another pastor added to the rationale for the change by bringing up personal evangelism. "Kennedy's plan for personal evangelism was not supposed to take away from the altar call, but it did. . . . Before we knew it, we had mixed our method, and now we don't know which way we are going."

One final remark: "Yes, there has been a shift. I have even recognized it in myself. I've seen that shift, and I think it's healthy. I'm 43 years old, and back in the Midwest we all preached the crisis experience as a cure-all for everything, even being a human being. Nearly any evangelist could preach me out of my religion. . . . The old-fashioned idea of the altar call just isn't doing it."

Consistently Barren Altars

This is a heartbreaking problem. One district superintendent volunteered his feelings about barren altars: "I have two widely known laymen, men of stature on my district who actually talked with me about going to headquarters to talk with the church officials about why we don't have more altar invitations in our churches. These men represent two different congregations, and neither of their churches is growing. They say they have talked with laymen from other churches who feel as they do."

These laymen who were unhappy with the limited number of altar calls in their services would not have found much comfort in the report of the pastor who said, "I try to give an altar call about half the time on Sunday mornings, and the altar is barren 80 percent of the time." Another pastor reported four seekers in five months.

Another man said, "We only have 10 or 12 seekers at a district camp meeting service. Why? I think it is because of the hardness of the people. No one has a burden much anymore. Everybody is so busy, we just never have enough time."

The most plaintive response on the barren altar came from a pastor in a well-known church in a well-known city. He and I have been friends for many years, and I know he was hurting when he told me how he felt about barren altars: "People in our church just accept the fact that no one comes to the altar much anymore. . . . We've talked about the barren altars in our church board meetings, and they just take it for granted and say times are different. . . . I don't really believe our people care much about building the kingdom of God. They just want to look after their families and make it to heaven themselves. It's sad. . . . I really thought they were going to turn down a plan I had to get full information on all the people moving into our section of the city. They said they had no time to call on them even if we did have the names and addresses."

Communion at the Altar

Although all of these pastors in slow-growing churches had at least 200 members, most of them were committed to the idea of Communion at the altar served by the pastor. But not all of their congregations are. One pastor said, "I would rather serve them Communion at the altar in shifts, but it takes more time, and I am afraid to try it."

Another man said, "We serve them in the seats like the Presbyterians and Church of Christ do, but I would much rather serve them at the altar. . . . Trouble is, my people wouldn't wait that long."

Another pastor who is determined to serve Communion at the altar, uses Sunday evenings for Communion. He does this four or five times per year.

Beyond the Altar

All of these pastors have some kind of training classes available with a variety of curricula from various Christian publishing houses. The problem in each church is the lack of new people and new converts to fill the classes. Perhaps an Ohio pastor said it for himself and the others: "We are doing the best we can. . . . Our people need a burden for souls. . . . It's my greatest concern." One of his colleagues had the last word: "I think the altar is one of our greatest assets if we can learn how to use it."

A closing word: After I finished reading all my notes from the interviews I had with these pastors, I sat back in my chair with my fingers locked behind my head, thinking and praying. We have the concept of the altar. We have these good men, excellent men. No one can fault their motives. How can we get their means and their motives together in an effective use of the altar? I'm not sure. But if we could, the results would revolutionize the church in one quadrennium.

DIVISION FIVE

Four Approaches to the Altar

Come home, come home.
Ye who are weary, come home.
Earnestly, tenderly Jesus is calling,
Calling, "O sinner, come home!"
—from the hymn "Softly and Tenderly"

13

A Cycle of Evangelism

ULTIMATELY, each pastor and congregation decides on the importance of the altar and how it is to be used in their local church. The altar is a tool as a spade is a tool. When the spade is used, it shines; and if it were human, it would have good feelings about itself. If the spade is left against the garden wall, creeping rust takes over. How and when the spade is used depends on whether or not someone with a garden is willing to exert the physical energy spadework requires.

And so it is with the altar. Success with the altar depends on the willingness of the pastor and the congregation to do the hard work it takes to recruit new people. The altar is used more often in the church with a constant flow of new people and growing number of children and teens than it ever can be in a congregation whose families are grown and few new people are attending. The magnetism of the altar will be increased in direct ratio to the ability of the church to draw people.

This idea of the church as a magnet attracting people works in different ways in different churches. All magnets don't look alike, but the pastor of every fast-growing church I interviewed had a clear idea of what he and his people were doing to provide their influx of new families. (1) All of these fast-growing churches used Christian celebrities for big events, but each pastor was quick to say these events of themselves did not build their churches. (2) Only one of the pastors I talked with had an organized calling program set for a certain night in the week. One pastor said home visitations after dark were dangerous even when they were made by appointment. He said the telephone was better. (3) Each of these pastors had scores of groups within his church who absorbed people in Christian fellowship and served as spiritual and social support groups. (4) Every one of these fast-growing churches had many special interest groups, all the way through the alphabet, from auto rebuilding clubs to a xylophone band. Their churches are centers of activity, day and night. (5) And two final notes: None of the services in these growing churches is allowed to become a boring litany of predictable churchly functions. Every service is the alive result of much thought about a variety of ways to meet the spiritual and social needs of people. Singing, handshaking, praying, listening, and responding are not just functions in a service. They are integral parts of a total picture of worship and evangelism. (6) There is spontaneity in all of these fast-growing churches, but nothing just happens. Effective pastors do great amounts of advance planning.

A Word of Explanation

Division Five is given to four different approaches pastors have actually used successfully in making their altars centers of spiritual activity. Each of these approaches has been hammered out on the anvil of experience by a real pastor in an actual assignment. It is not likely that any one of these approaches can, or should be, replicated somewhere else. But what these pastors have done may, hopefully, motivate us to make an adaptation that fits our local situation and our own approach to ministry.

Once the evangelism strategy has been determined by the pastor, then all that's left is to put the spade into the ground, again, and again, and again, fine-tuning our methods and techniques as we turn over the soil, plant a variety of seeds, weed out the undergrowth, and cultivate the garden. The following personal approaches to evangelism are based on discussions that I have recast for this manuscript. These pastors are not identified because of the promise of anonymity I made them before the interview began.

Rebuilding the Altar in an Old Church

"Pastor, I know your church has been around a long time and has suffered the pangs of moving twice to escape the ravages of metropolitan blight. As a result I also know your church went through some low, difficult years, which were made more painful by the tendency of the people to look back to their glory days. Tell me, how did you rebuild the altar into a place of victory and a positive tool in your evangelization when its importance had slipped? . . . Let's make it easy by starting with the question of the open altar."

"We had to cultivate a new attitude toward the altar as a place of love and victory instead of an unfriendly place where people publicly admitted their failures. If someone went to the altar, back in those early days, everyone wondered what he had done wrong. We had to get away from that. . . . The open altar is just part of the altar experience in our church. Some Sundays—like this morning when I preached on holiness—I have the open altar after the message. Other times I have it before the message. It just depends on how the Spirit leads me. The altar call is the same before or after the sermon; it's just for people who need to pray."

"You don't distinguish between the open altar and the altar call?"

"No. It's the same either way. . . . Years ago, I learned that people come to the altar for their own reasons, not mine. I also learned that people don't often come to the altar to pray about what I have preached on directly. What they have heard is different from what I thought I had preached. . . . A Spirit-filled sermon is like a 30-minute Rorschach blot psychologists use with their patients who are asked to tell a story about what they see in the inkblot. I believe people listen to a sermon and project on to it whatever their needs are. If, after trying, the sermon doesn't speak to any need they feel, it is just tuned out."

"Do you have good responses when the altar is opened after your sermon?"

"Almost always."

"Are you hedging?"

"Well, a little. The only time I have a reluctant response is when the sermon is strong."

"Strong?"

"Yes; forceful, a personal, direct kind of message."

"Give me an example."

"OK. When I preached a sermon recently on 'Judge not, that ye be not judged' [Matt. 7:1], I gave an invitation, but there was not much response. The people didn't know how to handle what I had said. It's strong stuff when you start talking about not judging. But over the next few Sundays there were several people at the altar who told me later they were there praying about issues that were awakened by the sermon on judging."

"I think you preached a series on divorce."

"Yes, but I didn't give any invitations; it's too traumatic. During those sermons is one of the few times I have broken down and wept publicly under my own preaching. Divorce is a terrible thing. . . . The congregation's response was terrific, but it didn't show up at the altar right at that time."

"Do you use this same approach to the altar call when you preach in a revival?"

"Yes. It works even in a small church. I know, because I only hold revivals in small churches for some specific reasons. They need me; my price is right—and there's one more important factor: They will let me come home for Sunday morning. I just won't be gone on Sunday morning, and our people know that."

"What do you mean, working in small churches?"

"Oh, yes, I got off the track, didn't I? On the first night of revival I preach on something that leads to an altar call and then publicly invite the chairman of the church board to come forward, representing the board members. And I ask the Sunday School superintendent to come and represent the teachers. I have soon dealt with the stigma problem, and it isn't long until some honest seekers join in the move toward the altar."

"Speaking of revivals, do you ever give your own invitations during revivals in your own church?"

"Yes, if the evangelist will allow me. . . . And I always do better than they would have done because the people know me and trust me, and my giving of the invitation is a tacit approval of the sermon. And sometimes the people need that, especially the new people."

"Is it ever a problem?"

"Oh, yes! Some evangelists have strong feelings about giving their own invitations. And when they do, I just back off. Dr. Greathouse let me give the invitations when he was with us. And it really worked well. In two minutes I could take what he had said profoundly and eloquently and reduce it down to size for our people. They had already heard his spirit. They saw him as a kind man. And they responded at the altar."

"What about workers during the altar service?"

"I have some people I can count on. And if people are moving forward—and I can usually tell who will come— these people know to move to their side. We believe everyone who comes to the altar wants help, and if the helper is the right kind of person, there is something therapeutic about laying your hand on someone's shoulder or arm. These altar workers are people with a good sense of the fitness of things."

"You don't call for all the Christians to come and pray around the altar?"

"Sometimes. The altar service is like everything else: Sameness is death. Our approach must have room for variety. So occasionally I just call for everyone to come. . . . Of course, there is not room for everyone, but lots of people do come forward."

"Your people—at least now—do not resist coming to pray?"

"Oh, my, no!"

"Did they when you first became their pastor?"

"Yes, some. It was a pretty staid church, and ... Of course, there was still a remnant of the idea that the altar was just for the bad guys, and the good guys either went forward to pray for the sinners, or they just sat there and watched to see how things went. That was bad! ... In an effort to loosen up the whole idea about using the altar, I often talked about sinners who could only come to the altar once, and after that they had to be a Christian to come."

"Well, now, tell me, what kinds of programs do you have to get the new Christians involved in the life of the church so that they feel like it's their church?"

A Cycle of Evangelism

"We have a cycle of evangelism that most of our people understand enough to support, although I'm sure not many could explain it in outline form. By that I mean our people understand it and help make the system work; they feel the vitality and aliveness in the Body without being able to identify all the bones in the structure."

"Is this cycle of evangelism for new people or new converts?"

It's the same both ways—new converts and new people. We work on both kinds of people at the same time."

"OK, tell me how it works."

"On paper it looks like a circle. We start in, first of all, to create a happy, positive atmosphere for people to feel the first time they enter our church, even our parking lots. This acceptance is triple-A: Acceptance, Anticipation, and Appreciation. This is top-drawer priority, a matter of first concern. ... Unless there is a spirit of radiant, happy optimism in the

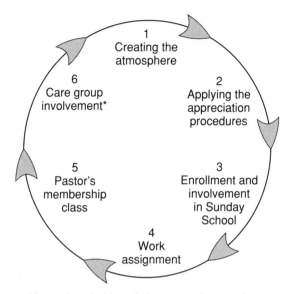

1
Creating the
atmosphere

6
Care group
involvement*

2
Applying the
appreciation
procedures

5
Pastor's
membership
class

3
Enrollment and
involvement
in Sunday
School

4
Work
assignment

*Somewhere in this cycle is a conversion experience,
an infilling of the Holy Sprit,
and/or a buying into the idea that "This is my church,"
according to the level of the new person's spiritual needs.

The Cycle of Evangelism

church, all of the activity programs are heavily discounted.
. . . I think a lot of people go to seminars and read books, then
start implementing programs in the same old negative, legal-
istic atmosphere that killed all the previous programs. Even
chrome-plated ideas fall flat unless the personality of the
church is positive and happy."

"I buy that. But how do you begin to create that kind of
spirit when there is not much to work with?"

It's not easy, especially if the people tend to be quarrelsome by habit. I read about a study once that concluded
that people who worked in factories, lived on the plains with
no sight of the mountains, and did not live near lakes or
oceans, tended to be more unhappy and quarrelsome than
those who did. I don't know if that is scientific or not, but I
believe it has a point."

"But how do you make the first small steps to create an accepting church with members who appreciate each other and anticipate all that is going on?"

I think you start by training good greeters and smiling ushers. Then get the church painted, cut the grass, and trim the shrubs—plant some if there aren't any. I think flowers are more important outside the church than they are inside. Get a new sign or fix up the old one. Make the sanctuary and classrooms spotlessly clean; you may even need to air out the place. Then start greeting the people yourself, as they arrive. Open some car doors; but never ask anyone how they feel unless you are ready to hear an organ recital. Just make positive, affirming statements that do not even call for a response. I never make anyone act friendly who doesn't want to be. Some people act sour just to get attention, but I never let on I notice. Then I have complete control of the pulpit. And that means I can preach in an inspiring, encouraging way, and not with harshness in a negative way. Little by little the personality of the church changes for the better; and once the spirit of happiness catches on, it develops a life of its own, and the church is on its way."

"Wow! That's a concept. But I know it's harder to do than it sounds."

"Yes, but it works. And I believe any pastor—I mean, *any* pastor—can do it, if he gets the concept in his mind and begins to work at it with all his heart. If the pastor himself isn't happy, the people never will be; but if the pastor is happy, the people can't resist his spirit forever."

"Well, . . . that's a lot to think about. After creating the spirit of happy, radiant optimism, what do you do next to win people and hold them?"

"The second thing we do is our set of immediate follow-up procedures. It's called Appreciation. If a new family attends our church on Sunday morning, they get a phone call of appreciation that afternoon, from a layman, not a pastor. If they attend at night, they get a call before they go to bed. It's a real surprise to most of these folks, especially in a big city like ours. These cities can be impersonal to the point of self-doubt and emotional pain."

"What else do you do?"

"Each new family gets a letter from the pastor and a phone call during the week from one of the pastors. Then we have a packet we drop off at their home. We try in all the ways we know to express our appreciation for their visit. Incidentally, this follow-up procedure depends entirely on our skills in getting these names, addresses, and telephone numbers. We don't depend alone on cards dropped into the offering plates. We have people assigned to work the foyer in search of new people. Some people in our congregation have a gift at this kind of thing!"

"Do people—visitors, that is—cooperate with this idea of signing up?"

"No! Not everyone. Some people don't even want to give us their name. Some will give their name because it is hard not to without being rude, especially since we are such nice people, but they just don't want to sign anything. That's OK with us. We don't push. If they come back a few times, the information leaks out anyhow. And incidentally, the suspicious person who is slow in giving information is usually someone who has been disappointed in some previous church connection. They respond better to our appreciation than most others when they finally get to the place where they are ready to identify themselves."

"But the end result of your appreciation program is good?"

"Oh, yes! Last year we had 260 new families who signed cards. That's an average of 5 families, or about 20 people per Sunday. We figure that 1 in 5 of these families is a good prospect for our kind of church. At the moment, of the 260 families, we have 50 or so who are attending with enough regularity to call this their church and refer to me as their pastor."

"This means a pastor who cleans up and airs out and shapes up his church and gets started on this appreciation program should expect five or six families to visit before he wins one for keeps."

"That's not far off; at least that's our experience."

"OK. What else?"

"The third rung in our circle is the Sunday School."

"The Sunday School? I don't hear people talking Sunday School like we used to. I thought most pastors were letting it maintain itself."

"We don't. In fact, we feel that Sunday School classes that are alive and well are one of our best tools in winning people and working them into the main fabric of the church."

"Why?"

"People don't commit to a church service regardless of how good it is. They don't even commit to a cause. They commit to a small group of people whom they have come to know and appreciate."

"Can you get adults to attend a Sunday School class?"

It's simple. As soon as a family shows the slightest continuing interest in our church, we enroll them in the classes; kids, teens, and adults. You know, you don't even have to attend to be enrolled. You could enroll the phone book if you wanted to. We enroll lots of people before they have ever attended a class. The enrollment just says to a Sunday School teacher, this couple or this child is a responsibility of yours. And our teachers follow through."

"Aren't Sunday School lectures dull?"

"They sure are; and that is why we don't have any adult classes with lecturing teachers. In fact, we had one or two, and their classes died. Our teachers have learned to teach relationally. They get discussion going. They always have some members of their class ready to speak up when things get slow. The big thing with us is exchange. Everybody needs some place where he can express honest doubt and not be criticized or judged, not even put down. It does people good to get a feeling out into the open and not be rejected for it. They need to be able to say that something doesn't make sense to them, or, 'What does such and such really mean? I don't understand it.' There are usually others who have their same doubt or concern. The place to doubt is in church or more specifically in a Sunday School class among Christian friends, not outside among fellow doubters who add fuel to the fire and put down the church."

"Well, well! Those are some refreshing thoughts."

"As a new person, I could attend church and think everyone has his problems worked out but me; not in Sunday School. Classes are for the hammering-out process. And another thing. Sunday School is our major social program. All of the social life in our church is by classes. It's a good system, and the people seem to thrive on it, even if it is old-fashioned. However, I must say that all of the people do not go for the idea of attending Sunday School classes. We try to find other ways of working them into the church, because it's easy to lose them in the cracks. Sometime I am going to have a telephone room in our church where laymen and pastors call people during the evening and on Saturday morning. I have a friend with a telephone room that is used 10 hours a week, primarily to keep uninvolved people from falling through the cracks and being lost."

"What's the fourth thing you do in your cycle of evangelism?"

"There is one thing that makes people feel they belong more than anything else, and that is a job. Everybody needs a place to work, something to do. In some churches you must sing in the choir, sit on the church board, or take up the offering—and that's OK—but we have lots of jobs, mostly short-term. In fact, the best jobs have an agreed beginning and end. The people know what they are getting into; otherwise it's like the job is forever. And resigning or changing it is hard. When I get someone to accept a job, he begins to think about this being his church."

"That's great! What's number five?"

"Number five is the church membership class. This is a pretty elaborate procedure with us. When you've joined our church, you know you've joined. They have been to the altar unless they are a transfer family. They have been around long enough to feel good about our church and their connection to it. Now comes the indoctrination part. We meet for six Sunday afternoons at 5:30, and I teach the class myself."

"Do you have any trouble getting people to commit for that many classes?"

"Not really. Of course we lose some. But those who stick it out for six weeks make mighty fine members. We cover doctrine, history, polity, and all the usual things. Then we invite everyone who has finished the class to the parsonage for dessert on Saturday night before they join on Sunday morning. This gives them a chance to see where the pastor and his family live, which is usually good. But we also have a sponsor present at this parsonage gathering for each new member or new family."

"You mean you have people assigned to look after each of these new families?"

"Right! It works like a charm. The sponsor checks on them, helps them with problems, prays with them, and in general does anything he can do to further their full entry into the life of our church and the advancement of their spiritual growth."

"What about singles? I notice you always talk about families."

"It's the same thing. A single is a very important person in a family unit of one. We don't treat singles as a different species but as persons. We have lots of singles."

"It looks like we're running out of time. Let's move on to number six."

"The sixth thing we do in our cycle of evangelism is to be sure every member is part of a care group. Usually the care group leader is their sponsor. Even when we have had 25 or 30 new members joining at once, we have had enough sponsors available from among the care group leaders to stand by each family."

"How do you get these care groups organized?"

"We break all the usual rules. We just appoint care group

leaders, and they invite the people they want to include into their care group. Then when we have new members, we ask an equal number of care group leaders to invite one of the new families into their groups. We don't pay any attention to geographic zones, because everybody drives, and everybody has a phone. These groups pray for each other, meet for Bible study, and serve as a support group for each other."

"Well, you must have one more phase in your cycle of evangelism, and I can guess what it is. By this time you have the new family fully engaged in maintaining the spirit of Christian optimism and goodwill that appealed to them in the first place."

"You're right; we practice life-style evangelism. It's the best for us by far. This means we must provide the people, new and old, with plenty of good things to talk about spiritually."

"Give me an example."

"Sure! One of the best things we have is the constant talk about our Work and Witness teams and their trips to mission fields. Last year we sent 60 people to Africa. And they came home talking to everyone who would listen. You don't go to Africa and then not talk about it. We had several families who turned to our church because they thought a church that sent that many people to Africa to help needy people, and raise all the money for the project, must be the kind of church they would like to know more about."

"Do you use celebrity concerts?"

"Yes, but for different reasons. They are not as popular as they used to be. They don't even draw the crowds. Unless they minister to the needs of our people, the congregation doesn't care much about them. They almost never bring in a new family that stays. Celebrities borrow families for an evening, but they never win anyone. What seems to work for us is a vital, vibrant spiritual atmosphere in our church, with structured opportunities for the people to know and work and learn with each other. With this kind of a garden to work in, the altar is a spade that never gathers rust."

A concluding word: This interview was chosen for inclusion in the study on the altar for several reasons. (1) The pastor has led a church in a great metropolitan area back to a radiant spirit of evangelism after it had fallen on hard times for more than a decade. They received more than 100 new members last year. (2) This pastor's methods are an update on the traditional approach to evangelism. (3) Everything this pastor does has positive overtones. His approach can be borrowed and adjusted to about any pastor and congregation who are motivated to be a fast-growing church.

14

From Reaction to Response

PASTOR, in my study of the altar and the altar call, I have tried to be open and honest, letting my work lead me where it will. I know you suffered spiritual shock on returning to the United States after more than a dozen years of missionary work in an isolated region, remote from any Christian cultural influences. I understand it was not worldliness or legalism, in either extreme, that you reacted to, but the confusion you saw and heard in the altar services."

"You are exactly right. As a kid growing up, I had a great appreciation for the altar. I went to it many times. It was the place of personal religious experience for me, including my call to be a missionary."

"What was the problem, then—I mean, when you got back home?"

"As I look back on it, I guess I couldn't adjust to the altar methods, for that is where I encountered most of my problems as a missionary doing deputation work. I came from a place where we could work a year to get one convert and be glad. Now what I saw in the church back home was confusing. The altar call and the prayer and talking around the altar was one of the most confusing things I had to face . . . especially in camp meetings, which is where we spent a lot of time that first summer back."

"How was it confusing?"

"I tried to figure out what it was all about, being away from the country so long. I saw the manipulation to get numbers, and that frustrated me. All of the concern for numbers disintegrated within me during our years away. We had concentrated on getting one convert who would stick. Then I was equally appalled at what happened after the people were kneeling at the altar. After the altar call was closed with that inevitable one more stanza or chorus, and once the people got to the altar, the confusion around them was so disconcerting that sometimes I would just go home. I did not like what I was doing, but I did know I was reacting honestly."

"Did things clear up after you got off the camp meeting trail and you settled down in a regular pastoral assignment?"

"Yes and no! I was still troubled. I needed to move from a reaction to a response, from being against something to being for something. I still loved the altar, and I believed in it; I just did not know yet how I was to use it for the glory of God. I wanted the altar to be the center of helpfulness for my people. I guess what happened to me over the next few years was more like a pilgrimage than some one great moment of spiritual insight, a pilgrimage highlighted by several very important 'aha!' moments of instantaneous learning."

"What was the first moment like?"

"When we got settled into our own church and the spiritual welfare of the people was my responsibility as the pastor, and I was no longer the guest missionary speaker, I determined not to allow the confusing kind of altar service I had reacted against ever to happen in my church. But that was negative; I needed the Holy Spirit to give me a positive response."

"What happened?"

"I began to come to grips with the fact that lots of people came to church hurting. On one level they were victorious because they had not given up their faith or turned against the theology of the Cross. But at another level they had problems, lots of problems. They were not always riding high. Everything was not always terrific: "saved; sanctified; praise the Lord, it's great to be a Christian!" People who always tried to project that kind of spiritual image could not mask the fact their families were disintegrating, their teens were using drugs, whole families were coping with the sordid results of teens who turned young love into sexual license. People who had lost their jobs, had shocking news about their health, and other sorts of things were so uptight they took out their frustrations on their families. The people they loved the most got hit the hardest. When I sat on the platform and looked into the faces of my people at both levels, the happy level and the hurting level, I saw the confusion that was echoed in my own spirit."

"That's a powerful insight. What happened next?"

"I did not aim for numbers. I thought I would be the pastor who always gave the low-key altar call and never had any guest speakers who put pressure on my people. But this was not the answer. I was still reacting. Then one Sunday morning, out of the clear sky, the words *family altar* came into my consciousness. I nearly stopped the service; in fact, I did set aside the order of worship. I moved to the pulpit and told the people what the Holy Spirit had brought to my mind as I sat praying for them just a few moments before."

"What did you say?"

"We are a church family, and we are going to have a *family altar* right now, here this morning, this very minute. There are some of you who want to come to the altar and pray about your own needs, right now. If you are in that group with needs and you want to pray, just stand where you are and come forward."

"And they came?"

"Yes. And the Lord gave me a new, positive feeling about the altar. I began to relax my own demands for the altar. I think our problem is what we demand of the altar, not what the Holy Spirit expects to do through that piece of furniture."

"Did this cure your altar call problem from then on?"

"Not exactly. I found a bit of resistance because the altar had a long history of negative images of spiritual and moral failure, which raised questions in the minds of the people when anyone but a child or a new person went forward. The people were wondering what the seeker was seeking, and why. The altar was a place to count, or not to count, or discount."

"I suppose you got past that feeling after a while?"

"I don't know if we ever get past it entirely because we've been conditioned for a long time. But I began to gather the people for family altar every Sunday morning."

"Did this become your altar call?"

"Oh, no! In fact, the family altar did not take the place of my own pastoral prayer. I think this is the weakness of the open altar in lots of churches; it takes the place of the pastoral prayer. I like the open altar, and I think it is good for the people to come, but I would not miss the pastoral prayer for anything—separate and on its own. The pastor leads his congregation in prayer; better still, he brings them to God through prayer. No one ever prays that prayer for me. I could have a dozen general superintendents and bishops in the service, but I would never ask any one of them to pray that prayer for me. That's my time with my people like no other time I ever have."

"Great! . . . But back to the family altar."

"Sometime during the service, when the Holy Spirit nudges me, I simply stand and tell them, 'It is time for the family altar. There is someone here who really needs to take a step forward and pray about your need.' . . . What surprised me, after the general resistance to the altar was behind me, was that the people actually came to church planning to come forward during the family altar—couples who needed to pray together, children who were having difficulties. God knows it is tough enough to serve Him in any teenager's world. . . . People came for healing."

"How did you deal with all these needs?"

"Many a Sunday, I would just go down to that altar, lay my hands on the people, give a scripture that had come to mind. And to my amazement, I found that people had been healed."

"You mean physical healing?"

"I mean healing in all the ways God heals: bodies, memories, emotions, healing from sin, cleansing. I found that people had been saved and sometimes sanctified."

"This then became your altar call?"

"Oh, no! The altar call at the end of the sermon was another matter. The family altar did not stop me from inviting people to the altar at the close of my message. I often gave an altar call at the end of the sermon—many times. And because of the relaxed nature of my attitude toward the altar, I found more people ready to come at the close of the sermon than I used to when I was uptight about the invitation. I think the point of light God gave me was a new, relaxed attitude toward the altar. I learned to let the Holy Spirit make the altar call and the family altar what He wanted them to be."

"It is amazing to me that you find the open altar and the altar call supporting each other. Some people feel they should not be used in the same service."

"No! My experience is just the opposite. I guess it just helps to prove that each of us has to find a way to work with the altar that fits us and is blessed of the Holy Spirit. If someone believes these two approaches to the altar discount each other, then I'm sure they do, for them, but not me."

"What else can you tell me about your way of using the altar as a means of grace?"

"Another thing I found—and I could be corrected in this matter—was the willingness of the people to come forward immediately at the close of the sermon, if they were coming at all. I never extend an invitation for long. Our people know this, and maybe that is why they move on out to the altar soon, not later. They know I am not going to make a pull, or whatever. Last year I was in the South Pacific in a Baptist church that had no altar. I was quick to ask for an altar where people could come and pray, and they quickly adjusted. The people accepted the idea and began to appreciate it. I guess it was like Dr. Criswell putting in the altar at Dallas First Baptist. I think the people will respond in any setting when they feel the preacher has a relaxed attitude about the altar, is open, honest, and kind. The chances of the people responding are far greater than they are for a pastor who is hung up over his own possibility of failure and turns on the people in an accusing way to get them to admit their failure so that he won't have to admit his."

"Any other word? What about specific invitations?"

"I don't discount specific invitations. But I have found that a wide-open net seems to cover more needs than a narrow one. I don't want to miss the person who needs to be saved or sanctified, but I also don't want to miss the man or woman who is crushed over a personal problem they can't very well share with anyone except the Lord."

"What about altar workers?"

"I try to select our altar workers. I have specific people whom I have trained. They know when to move to the altar. And this even encourages others to come. Our workers come with their Bibles, asking God for wisdom and how to be specific in helping the people with whom they pray, not to make them embarrassed, but to make them feel they have a partner praying with them who cares and knows what to do to be helpful. . . . At least that is what I try to do with our workers. . . . Unnecessary chatter around the altar just drives me bats. Maybe it's a hangover from some former era. But I really do believe in the sacredness of what is happening around the altar when people have brought their needs to God. Chatter around the altar is the devil's poison gas."

"What about crisis and process?"

"I believe in both. However, I think kneeling at the altar may be the first step toward personal knowledge of Jesus Christ as Lord, but sometimes there are other steps before a new Christian has what John Wesley called the inner witness of the Spirit."

"That's interesting, because Dr. Bresee made up his mind to be a Christian while his pastor was visiting him in the store where he worked. He went to church that Friday night and said he could hardly wait to go to the altar. But then he also reports that he was saved two days later, during a Methodist class meeting held after the Sunday morning service. And Finney had much the same journey into a crisis experience that satisfied his faith and changed his life forever."

"I have a friend who believes that most people are finally converted, brought to a satisfying faith in Christ's blood for salvation, during the follow-up classes after a seeker has been to the altar. He believes a seeker cannot participate in several hours of teaching on the meaning of saving faith without getting in completely or dropping out. And with the dropouts, we start all over again."

"Makes sense."

"That is why I am absolutely amazed at any pastor who works a full year and reports no new converts by profession of faith who join the church. If a pastor has any approach to the altar that he really believes in, I just believe that the Holy Spirit will honor his efforts with some kind of results that are visible."

A concluding word: This interview was chosen for inclusion in this study because it demonstrates the importance of the pastor's attitude in his approach to the altar. Also, his story reminds us that reacting is always negative and responding is always positive. The ministry of every effective pastor in this study is responsive to the needs of his people and not reactive against them.

15 ≡

A Bold Approach

PASTOR, I'm doing a study on the altar, the altar call, and the altar service, including whatever else relates to it."

"You mean, you are doing a study on how we win people to Christ and then get them into the church and motivated to become part of the ministry in winning more people to Christ?"

"Yes. But there is more to it. I have come to you for a special reason. I have studied your statistics and awards, but I want to know your whole concept on winning the unchurched. It seems people are coming to believe the altar is just one segment—an important segment, if you will—but just one part of the process of evangelism. There was a time when we felt the primary work of the church was to get people under the sound of gospel preaching, and then the altar experience would take care of the rest, and we would go out to get in more people. The altar was a cure-all, an end in itself."

"Yes, I grew up in a congregation that believed and practiced that approach to evangelism. The number at the altar, the persuasiveness of the evangelist, the power of the conversion experience, and the experience of entire sanctification were the major factors to watch."

"Right! I still believe that very much. But I also see men like you, in the holiness tradition, who have broadened the altar experience to include important factors both before and after the altar. You have been singularly successful in winning unchurched people to the Lord. What is your philosophy, your method? What has the Holy Spirit led you to do?"

"Those are important questions. But let me begin with one basic thought: Unless I, the pastor of this specific church, have my own concept of how to win the unchurched to Christ and the church, fundamentally in my own mind and heart so that I really believe it and my people can feel that I really believe it, I will never be effective."

"What if your approach were inept? Obviously it isn't, but what if it were? Would it still be effective if you believed in it?"

"Even if my approach were inept, I believe God would overcome my ineptness—as certainly He does—if I really believe in what I am doing to reach the unchurched and work at it every week. I tried for too long to get off the hook with God because I was not as clever as some other pastor who had a faster-growing church than I did, or had a more supportive congregation than I had, or even a more spiritual congregation than I had."

"You believe the place of beginning is to have an approach to winning the unchurched you really believe in and can work at comfortably on your own terms."

"Right! I guess it is better to use somebody else's approach than to use no approach at all. It may be a point of beginning, but before long the other person's approach will be so fully adapted to your own style and personality that it will become your own. What is sad, even tragic, is to see some man called of God, educated in the ways of the church, but drifting through an entire year without any wheat in the bin. A farmer with no harvest has jeopardized himself as a farmer. He won't expect to stay in the business very long if things aren't turned around. As a pastor, I can be doing the functions of evangelism, but if I don't have any harvest, I'm in trouble. I can blame the weather or the bugs for my lack of harvest—and those may be valid reasons for my failure—but it is still failure, and I can't keep farming very long like that. God's plan is to help me overcome the blight and to give me enough moisture for some kind of harvest—very few farmers have a total failure, although very few I know are ever fully satisfied with their harvest every year. What makes a farmer successful is a concept of farming that he works at diligently year after year with varying levels of annual success. . . . But being a farmer is different from being a pastor. Farmers aren't voted on by their harvest hands. The pastor has to bring the congregation along with him, and he does that as they begin to grasp the sincerity and love with which he speaks when he talks about reaching the unchurched and as they begin to see he has a plan that makes sense. The first thing you know, some of the people will begin to share his conviction. Then more and more of them will get on board, and his approach begins to be the approach of the congregation; corporate faith has begun to work!"

"That's great! Tell me now, what is the approach to evangelism that has you and your people motivated?"

At this point in our interview, the pastor left his seat and walked over to his desk, where he pulled a drawing out of a drawer that looked like the drawing below.

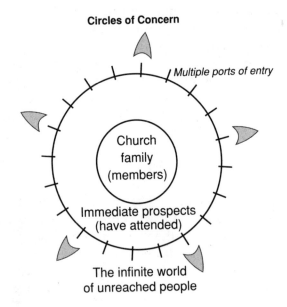

Circles of Concern

Multiple ports of entry

Church
family
(members)

Immediate prospects
(have attended)

The infinite world
of unreached people

"Those three circles represent all the people our church might ever influence."

"There's no third circle on the drawing; it has no border."

"Right you are! It is infinitely wide; it has no border. We believe there is no one we might not reach with the gospel. But that's not the point."

"I'm sorry; go ahead."

"The little hash marks (/) represent all the ports of entry people might use for ever coming to our church the first time. These may include special events, curiosity, an invitation, or whatever. The main thing is to get them here the first time and send them home with a hankering to come again. This hankering depends on the atmosphere they feel here, the openness of our people, whether or not the new family feels they could enjoy this church or ever have a sense of belonging. No joining! That's the furthest thing from their minds when they first come."

"What's next?"

"I believe that salvation is not limited to time and place. Sunday mornings at 11:00 and Sunday evenings at 6:00 are not the only times the Holy Spirit does His work. One of the most fruitful revivals we ever had did not include a Sunday. That meeting taught me that God is not tied down to Sundays. . . . And He's not tied down to places, sacred as they may be."

"What do you mean?"

"I went through a reaction to the altar I saw when I was just a young man. To watch our church, you would have thought God was only open for salvation business at 12 noon and 9 P.M. on Sundays during the singing of certain kinds of songs. When I graduated from Nazarene Theological Seminary, I went out determined to win people through personal evangelism, and the altar would only be a confirming place for the important work that we had done somewhere else. I was tempted to see myself as a person others rejected because my approach to winning the unchurched was not focused on the public altar. Then the church shifted to the personal approach under the Kennedy idea from Florida. But that didn't last long. I think now we may be drifting. And I don't mean that in a derogatory sense. I'm just concerned."

"Was this when you worked out your own approach?"

"Yes, and it has proved to be God's plan for us."

Let's move ahead. You've got some new people through your ports of entry into circle number two. Does that mean these people are now your responsibility? Or, at least, now they are live prospects?"

"Yes. They are now friends of the church. Since most of our people are unchurched or belong to that gray category of people some church has forgotten, I am continually concerned for them to be saved or to be spiritually awakened."

"How does that happen?"

"Anytime, anyplace, but usually right here in this church. It's important to remember that we have a two-pronged work going at the same time. While we are winning new people to Christ, we are deepening the Christians who have already been converted but have an unstructured faith. But for now, let's talk about new converts."

"Good. First things first."

"To get away from the idea of a stigma about the altar, we always have an open altar. Really, there isn't any other kind. People come forward for their own reasons, not for mine. Once when I was a youth pastor, Paul Martin gave me a case of spiritual depression when he preached on holiness when I had three teenagers in a revival service for the first time in their lives. They played on a baseball team I coached. I had worked and schemed for weeks to get them there. And I thought the sermon on sanctification would ruin it all. But I was wrong. When the invitation was given, all three of them went forward, and they are still in the church today. That incident taught me that people go to the altar for their own reasons."

"Do you have your open altar before the sermon or afterward?"

"Always before, never afterward, and I'll tell you why. At

the close of every sermon, I make an appeal for people to accept Christ. I just ask them to stand where they are, if they would really like to be a Christian. It's my version of what Billy Graham does when he invites people to stand in front of the platform at the close of his sermons."

"Do they stand?"

"Oh, yes! Lots of them. And at every service. I don't know when I have given an invitation and no one has stood."

"Then what?"

"I pray the sinner's prayer with them and ask them to repeat it after me. This does two things. It takes the sinner to the point of accepting Christ, but it also shows our people something about leading a soul to Christ. I often have people tell me that they talked to their friend about Jesus, and when they thought the friend was ready, they just prayed the sinner's prayer with them like I do on Sundays. When they see me do it, it helps them believe they can."

"Then?"

"I publicly ask one of our pastors to go and stand in front of the pulpit. I identify him and tell the people why he is there. Then I tell the people who are standing not to leave the sanctuary until they have come to this pastor for a word of instruction, a prayer, and a very important piece of paper each of them must have."

"Do they come?"

"Oh, yes, all of them. I don't think anyone ever leaves without coming forward."

"What is on the paper?"

"This is their very first Bible study. It is captioned 'Welcome into God's Family.' There are two scriptures to read, 1 John 1:9 and John 1:12. Then the remainder of the sheet outlines the four important steps in getting started: (1) Baptism—this Sunday evening. We make a lot out of baptism on the authority of the New Testament. We baptize new converts almost every Sunday night before the service begins. We only missed two Sunday nights last year. All of the other Sunday nights, there were people to be baptized. (2) New

Christian's Class. This is Basic Christianity 101. There are nine consecutive sessions that meet during the Sunday School hour to cover nine important subjects. Since we have double services now, people can attend either hour. And if they miss a class, they can make it up on the next cycle. But we are strong on attendance in these classes. They are a must! (3) Pastor's Welcome Class. This class lasts 2½ hours and is set for the second and fourth Wednesday evenings of the month from 7:00 to 9:30. We also offer it once a quarter on Saturday mornings. It is usually in this class that people nail down their decision and really experience Christ in saving grace. When I spot people who are hung up, I meet with them privately in my study. (4) Home Bible Lessons. There are eight lessons in this series to be completed at home and brought each week to the New Christian's Class."

"That's no small program: (1) Baptism, (2) New Christian's Class, (3) Pastor's Welcome Class, and (4) Home Bible Lessons."

"But it's not too much. Becoming a Christian is an important matter, and we want to be sure these new converts are well on their way."

"What about sanctification?"

"We believe very much in sanctification. We teach it as a crisis experience as it's taught in the Bible. But we also focus on holiness as a way of life. It is more than a second blessing, or a second experience, alone. Not only must we be filled with the Holy Spirit, but also we must show the fruit of the Spirit in daily living. There is crisis; but, friend, there must also be a lifelong pursuit. Our call to holiness is a continuing call that starts with cleansing and an infilling of the Holy Spirit and goes on for a lifetime."

"Let's get back to the invitations and open altar on Sunday morning. Your approach is not traditional; some people would even have questions about your invitation."

"I understand; and I expect this criticism. That was something I had to die out to when I was hammering out my plan. . . . But I am interested in outcomes, not the preservation of traditional means. And the thing we have going for us are all the changed lives, saved and sanctified people who are in Christ, and it shows. All of our detractors are from outside. In their fear of compromise some people see any change from the traditional as bad. I understand, and I don't blame them. But I also have no self-doubt about what we are doing. God has given us a job to do, and we believe we are doing it in harmony with the Bible and our church. We are getting more people saved and sanctified than we ever dared to think about before we started this approach to evangelism."

"Well, your method works; no one can deny that. Thank you for telling me your story of evangelism."

A concluding word: This interview was chosen for inclusion in this study because it demonstrates the variety and flexibility available to pastors who want to launch out with bold, new ideas in using the many effective ways there are for winning people to Christ and the church. This pastor has taken the Billy Graham approach to citywide evangelism and localized it for his own church. And it works.

16

Traditional Is Beautiful

PASTOR, I have preached enough times in your church to know how you feel about the altar and the altar call, and how important you feel the altar is in your ministry. In fact, I think you and I share the same wavelength when it comes to evangelism. But I need some help. Tell me how the altar fits into the total program of evangelism in your church."

"Sure."

"For an easy start, tell me how you use the open altar and the altar call so that they do not work against each other."

"I use both of them regularly. We have an open altar every Sunday morning with the exception of revival. I think the evangelist needs every advantage I can give him. I don't want to use up his time with the open altar, and I don't want to run the risk of the open altar taking something away from the altar call. There is one downside to the open altar, however, that I don't seem to know how to eliminate. We have too many of the same people who come every Sunday. And I've always noticed that the closer the people are to the altar, the more likely they are to come—the front, the transepts, the choir; not many, if any, come from the back. For the sake of the open altar, I'm glad we don't have a balcony. But I believe in it. I'm glad somebody thought up this marvelous means for helping people. You can put me down on the side of the open altar."

"What about the altar call after the sermon?"

"We have an altar call after the sermon every Sunday morning of the world, whether or not the sermon is evangelistic, and even if we have a visiting speaker."

"How do you do it?"

"First, let me say I don't know if there is as big a difference as we think there is between worship and evangelism. I think every service is a worship service. But sometimes I preach with more of an evangelistic thrust than at other times. The same shepherd who feeds the sheep also brings in the ones who are lost."

"Right. But tell me how you end the service on Sunday mornings."

"I pray at the end of the sermon. And while I am praying, a mixed quartet comes to stand behind me at the pulpit. When I say, 'Amen,' the pianist strikes a soft chord, and the quartet begins to sing an old hymn, not usually an invitation hymn but a song that conjures memory, such as 'My Jesus, I Love Thee,' or 'What a Friend We Have in Jesus.' It's easy for a mixed quartet to sing because they use the notes printed in the hymnbook. They don't need a special arrangement. Then I step back to the pulpit after their first verse and suggest that there must be people there who need to pray before we go home. I structure what I say to the focus of the sermon. Then I ask the quartet to repeat the same stanza again while people come to pray. We have had seekers every Sunday for years. The invitation is a very important part of our worship service."

"That's great!"

"We also have an invitation at night. We are just consistent. You can't tell who is present in any service. People need help, and we want to give them the opportunity to find that help at our altar."

"Is there any stigma? I keep hearing about this from some pastors."

"Oh, no! The altar is an accepted means of grace in our

church and is appreciated by those who go forward and those who don't."

"How many new members do you receive each year?"

"Usually 50 or so. Our goal, or norm, is about 1 member each Sunday, year in and year out. Some years we receive more than 50 but seldom less."

"If you are going to receive enough new people into the family of the church to win 50 or more per year as members, you must have a good system for recruiting first-time visitors."

"Well, we are old-fashioned. We still believe in visitation evangelism."

"Really? Not many people major on that anymore. How do you do it?"

"It works two ways with us. We train teams of threes who do actual evangelism in the homes every week. They gather at the church for prayer, get their assignment, go to the home, and then come back to the church with their report."

"Do they win people to the Lord?"

"Oh, yes! We use the Kennedy plan that was reworked and, I think, improved by our headquarters people. We present the plan of salvation from the Bible and pray people through right in their homes. But we do not consider the task finished until the new convert comes to the altar on Sunday morning. The team of three who prayed with the new convert in the home last Monday night gathers around the convert at the altar on the next Sunday to confirm his experience with the Lord. These are great times."

"What about the second kind of visitation you mentioned?"

"I don't think everyone has the gift of evangelism. Some people are too self-conscious to present the plan of salvation to strangers; but we still have a place for them. The second phase of our visitation is organized through the Sunday School classes. Outreach and follow-up are important functions of the classes. They don't meet on Monday nights with the home evangelists, but they have their assignments and follow through and report back to their teacher or to the evangelism committee of their class."

"You really have this approach working, don't you?"

"Yes, and it's because I believe in it. I'm sure younger, more innovative pastors than I am could do a better job than we do. But we just keep working away at it year after year. When we can get them saved, we enroll them in our Discipling Class for six months, then we graduate them into the Pastor's Membership Class, and finally receive them into the church. When they come through this process, they usually stick."

"So all your visitation work—both kinds—is done by trained teams; and all calls are made by appointment."

"Yes. We really couldn't call in homes any other way. People are afraid of unannounced visitors at their front door."

"Where do revivals fit into your approach to evangelism?"

"Revivals are very important to us. We usually have three a year, Wednesday over Sunday."

"Three a year!"

"Yes, fall, spring, and summer. Sometimes we don't have a fall revival because of our lay retreat program."

"How does that work?"

"From August to October we have a series of retreats that cover about all ages of young people and adults in various categories. We have retreats for teens, young adults, singles, young married, men, women, and so on. It costs the church a bundle, but it really produces spiritual results."

"I can't believe this. I never heard about your retreat program before."

"You should; one of your faculty members is one of our favorite speakers. He understands people, and he is always interesting. But back to the system. The group pays for the entertainment of their speaker and the cost of his travel. They do this with one or two offerings. Then the church picks up the tab for the speaker's honorarium."

"And I know you are always generous. But what about room and board for the laymen?"

"That is their responsibility. Some groups love to cook their own meals, while other groups prefer a hotel. We leave that up to them. And they pay for their own room. But it's not expensive. We keep the cost down."

"Where do you, as the pastor, fit into all of this long retreat program—from August to October—more than two months?"

"Oh, I attend all of the retreats, except I come home for Sunday morning. They stay through Sunday noon."

"Are you afraid their absence hurts your church? There must be Sunday School teachers among them. And then that absence makes your Sunday morning attendance smaller."

"I suppose, but the spiritual values far outweigh the liabilities. Some of our best evangelism is done in these retreats, often in the closing service on Sunday morning. We will have more than 400 of our people enrolled in these retreats each fall, including the church board. How else could you get more than 400 people in that many consecutive services?"

"I know about your spring revival, for I have been your evangelist twice. I know your weeknight services are well attended, but what about your summer revival? That's new to me."

"It's just like the fall and spring revivals. We call an evangelist and a singer and go to work at having revival."

"Do the people come?"

"Sure, sometimes better than in the fall or spring. The children are out of school, and the family pace is usually a little slower. Oh, yes! There is something else. For the last several years we have called a children's evangelist for each of our regular revivals. The children have their own meetings in the Family Center, while the teens and adults are in the sanctuary. The children love it. The parents love it for their children. Sunday School teachers like the special services for their children. It just works beautifully, and we plan to keep on having these simultaneous revivals for children and adults."

"That's a terrific idea. What other surprises do you have for me? You are the most innovative traditionalist I know."

"We do have one other thing that relates to revival. Every August, when the church needs a spiritual lift, we bring in a preacher and singer for a special day. We call it 'August Revival Sunday.' We have used the same preacher and singer each year for nearly a decade. We like both men very much. They are the kinds of men who are easy to have back again and again, but they would be hard to slate for a full revival because of their schedules. The crowds build on the good experience the church has had with them on all their previous visits. And the results are always good. We plan to keep on with our August Revival Sunday each year."

"I can see that revivals and the altar call are really important to you."

"They're hard work. Sometimes I sweat a revival out. Not every revival is of equal value."

"But you still believe in them."

"I couldn't get on without several revivals each year."

A concluding word: This interview was included in this study because it demonstrates the continuing effectiveness of traditional approaches to evangelism. There is nothing new in what this pastor does. Just that he does it, year in and year out, in good times and bad. He has proved that traditional altar evangelism works.

Summary and Predictions

We have come now to the end of our sojourn with the altar. We began with Noah. Now we are ready to think about congregations yet unformed and churches not yet constructed. However, before we move on, there are several statements that can be made in summary:

1. The kneeling altar is an American contribution to evangelism that became universally accepted in Methodism during the years of its greatest evangelistic fervor. If the Methodists were John Wesley's children, then the holiness churches of today are his grandchildren who have inherited the altar and made it an important place of encounter with God.

2. The altars in the Old Testament were places of sacrifice, gratitude, obedience, refuge, and praise, which are reflected in the modern uses of the kneeling altar where people find forgiveness, cleansing, and healing, and where they make commitments to God and to each other.

3. Christ is our ultimate Altar who sanctifies the gift. Through Him we have access to God, who meets all our needs. The kneeling altar in our churches is nothing more than a convenient place to pray, to receive Him as Lord of our lives, and to reaffirm our relationship with Him at special times of need and on occasions for public expression of gratitude. Actually, we do both. The altar is the place where human weakness and divine strength intersect.

4. In Peter and Paul we have the best New Testament models of preaching for decision. When Peter finished his message at Pentecost, the people did not clap; they asked what they should do to be saved.

5. The long night of the church was followed by the first streaks of a new dawn in Luther's justification by faith, Cal-

vin's free grace, Arminius' free will, and the personal religious experience of the Pietists. Although Wesley, Whitefield, and Edwards never gave public invitations for sinners to come forward for prayer, their evangelistic methods were the forerunner of the kneeling altar and the altar call.

6. The altar and the altar call came of age in the 19th century under Asbury and the Methodist mourner's bench, aided by Finney and the anxious seat. Phineas Bresee and the Nazarene altar became a symbol of glory in his ministry as a pastor-evangelist in the First Church of the Nazarene in Los Angeles. His love of the altar was typical among holiness leaders nationwide.

7. The love of the holiness people for the altar is demonstrated in their sensitivity to issues and concerns that may threaten its purposes and importance.

The Future of the Altar

This point in the study of the altar calls for predictions on where we are going in the use of the altar and the altar call. It is dangerous to make predictions; time may prove their folly. However, I was greatly impressed by a classroom discussion led by Dr. Fitch at the Pacific School of Religion. He said the task of studying the past was not complete unless we had the courage to make predictions on the basis of where we have come from and where we are. Without appearing to presume on my limited understanding, there are some predictions that can be made.

1. Love of the altar will not be abated in the foreseeable future. Concern for the altar is deeply rooted in the heritage of evangelical churches.

After 250 years, the Methodists went back to Aldersgate Street to celebrate the conversion of John Wesley. With Queen Elizabeth among the notables present from around the world, the Methodists brought in an altar for the outdoor service, which was set for the purpose of remembering the conversion of one man whose evangelism changed the history of England. Wesley's outdoor preaching paved the way for the Methodist camp meeting. His itinerant system opened the way for the concept of the circuit-riding preacher. And his strong preaching for decisions opened the way for the altar and the altar call. It would take a radical change of direction for Nazarenes to neglect their love affair with the altar.

2. Since barren altars are the biggest obstacle against keeping our love of the altar alive, we will face this problem by better training of pastors on effective use of the invitation.

Billy Graham is the best example of a nationally known preacher who makes the invitation an integral part of his ministry. Everyone goes to his services expecting him to give an invitation. People expect him to talk about the invitation at the beginning of his sermon, during the sermon, and at the conclusion. They are familiar with his pattern. They know counselors are trained to help seekers. They understand the main purpose of the service is to make an invitation. People would be disappointed if he did not. And everyone expects people to go forward when Billy invites them. An altar is not appropriate or practical in his big arena meetings. But Dr. Graham is a member of the Dallas First Baptist Church, where Dr. Criswell has made the altar an integral part of his ministry.

3. There will be more variety and ingenuity in the use of the altar. The stereotype of hard-line exhortations will continue to give way to a loving call after the fashion of our Lord here on earth. Jesus despised sin, but He loved sinners, and His love came through. The only people Jesus openly rejected were the legalists and the self-righteous.

While Bill Draper was our pastor, he gave an invitation morning and evening every week. And he always did it the same way: by suggesting he would like to walk down from the platform to stand at the altar while a hymn was being sung, and he would welcome anyone for any reason who would like the pastor to pray with him before he left the service. As I remember, there were always people who came forward. We knew he would give an invitation. We expected him to come down to our level for meeting us. We believed he genuinely loved us. And when we had needs, it seemed like a good idea to have him pray for us at the altar. Pastors who develop their own loving style of inviting people to the altar will continue to be effective in its use.

4. The future of the altar in growing churches is reassuring. Every pastor I interviewed from a fast-growing church loves the altar and uses it effectively. These men will continue to be creative in their use of the altar. The open altar will go through variations and may or may not endure under the methods now used. But there will always be flexibility in methods supported by conservatism in theology among the churches who have found ways to communicate with the secular culture of today. There is no reason to be skeptical of colleges, universities, seminaries, and other preacher training institutions. They love the altar. The highest administrators in the church love the altar. In college revivals, faculty are the first ones forward to pray with seekers. Missionaries build their lives around all the altar symbolisms, even in the most remote regions of the earth. Now is not the time to second-guess each other. Now is not the time to be skeptical of one another. Now is the time to reaffirm our commitment to all the altar is and ever can be under Spirit-anointed leadership.

Bibliography

Arnett, Dessie Ash, et al. *Methodist Altars.* Charleston, W.Va.: Private publication, Jarrett Printing Co., 1956.

Asbury, Francis. *Journal and Letters of Francis Asbury.* Nashville: Abingdon, 1958.

Atkinson, John. *Centennial History of American Methodism.* New York: Phillips and Hunt, 1884.

Autrey, C. E. *Basic Evangelism.* Grand Rapids: Zondervan Publishing House, 1959.

Bader, Jesse M. *Evangelism in a Changing America.* St. Louis: Bethany Press, 1957.

Bangs, Nathan. *History of the Methodist Episcopal Church.* New York: T. Mason and G. Lange, 1840.

Beardsley, Frank G. *A History of American Revivals.* Boston: American Tract Society, 1904.

Belden, A. D. *George Whitefield: The Awakener.* London: Rockliffe, 1953.

Booth, William. *The Founder Speaks Again.* London: Salvation Army Press, 1960.

Bready, John Wesley. *England Before and After Wesley.* London: Hodder and Stoughton, 1939.

Brickley, Donald P. *Man of the Morning: The Life and Work of Phineas F. Bresee.* Kansas City: Nazarene Publishing House, 1960.

Cross, Whitney R. *The Burned-Over District: The Social and Intellectual History of the Enthusiastic Religion in Western New York, 1800-1850.* Ithaca, N.Y.: Cornell University Press, 1950.

Dallimore, Arnold A. *George Whitefield: The Life and Times of the Great Evangelist of the Eighteenth-Century Revival.* Westchester, Ill.: Cornerstone Books, 1979.

Dalton, James S. "The Kentucky Camp Meeting Revivals of 1797-1805, as Rites of Initiation." Ph.D. diss., University of Chicago, 1973.

Downey, James Cecil. "The Music of American Revivalism." Ph.D. diss., Tulane University, 1968.

Ellis, William T. *Billy Sunday: The Man and His Message.* Philadelphia: John E. Winston Co., 1914.

Finney, Charles G. *Lectures on Religion.* New York: Fleming Revell, 1868.

———. *Memoirs.* New York: Fleming Revell, 1876. (Finney and Father Nash on pages 118-35.)

"The Function of Worship in the Religion of Israel." In *The Interpreter's Bible* 1:340.

Gilleson, Lewis W. *Billy Graham: The Man and His Message.* Greenwich, Conn.: Fawcett Publications, 1954.

Girvin, E. A. *Phineas F. Bresee: A Prince in Israel.* Kansas City: Nazarene Publishing House, 1916.

225

Green, Bryan. *The Practice of Evangelism*. New York: Charles Scribner's Sons, 1959.

Harding, William Henry. *Finney's Life and Lectures*. Grand Rapids: Zondervan Publishing House, 1956.

High, Stanley. *Billy Graham: The Personal Story of the Man, His Message, and His Mission*. New York: McGraw-Hill Book Co., 1956.

Hills, A. M. *Life of Charles G. Finney*. Cincinnati: Office of God's Revivalist, 1902.

"History of the Early Church." In *The Interpreter's Bible* 7:176.

Jackson, Thomas. *Memoirs of the Rev. Charles Wesley*. London: Epworth Press, 1848.

Johnson, Charles A. *The Frontier Camp Meeting: Religion's Harvest Time*. Dallas: Southern Methodist University Press, 1955.

Lacy, Benjamin. *Revivals in the Midst of the Years*. Richmond, Va.: John Knox Press, 1943.

Latourette, Kenneth Scott. *A History of Christianity*. New York: Harper Brothers, 1953.

Lawson, J. G. *Deeper Experiences of Famous Christians*. Anderson, Ind.: Warner Press, 1911.

Luccock, Halford. *The Acts of the Apostles*. New York: Harper and Brothers, 1942.

———. *The Story of Methodism*. New York: Abingdon, 1949.

McLoughlin, William, Jr. *Billy Graham: Revivalist in a Secular Age*. New York: Ronald Press, 1960.

———. *Modern Revivalism: Charles Finney to Billy Graham*. New York: Ronald Press, 1959.

———. *Revivals, Awakenings, and Reform: An Essay on Religion and Social Change in America, 1607-1977*. Chicago: University of Chicago Press, 1978.

Moore, E. C. *Spread of Christianity in the Modern World*. Chicago: University of Chicago Press, 1927.

Murray, Iain H. *The Invitation System*. London: Banner of Truth Trust, 1968.

Nagler, Arthur Wilford. *Pietism and Methodism*. Nashville: Publishing House of the Methodist Episcopal Church South, 1918.

Neve, J. L. *History of Christian Thought*. Philadelphia: Muhlenberg Press, 1946.

Nevin, J. W. *The Anxious Bench*. Chambersburg, Pa.: Weekly Messenger, 1843.

Nirbt, Carl. "Pietism." In *New Schaff-Herzog Encyclopedia of Religious Knowledge*, edited by Samuel M. Jackson, 9:59.

Nottingham, Elizabeth K. *Methodism and the Frontier: Indiana Proving Ground*. New York: Columbia University Press, 1941.

Olive, Howard Goodlett. "The Development of the Evangelistic Invitation." Master's thesis, Southern Baptist Theological Seminary, 1958.

Olmstead, Clifton E. *History of Religion in the United States*. Englewood Cliffs, N.J.: Prentice Hall, 1960.

Peters, John L. *Christian Perfectionism and American Methodism.* New York: Abingdon Press, 1956.

Pocknee, Cyril. *The Christian Altar in History and Today.* London: Armowbray and Co., 1963.

Porter, Ellen Jane Lorenz. "A Treasure of Camp Meeting Spirituals." Ph.D. diss., Union Graduate School, 1978.

Purkiser, W. T. *Exploring Our Christian Faith.* Rev. ed. Kansas City: Beacon Hill Press of Kansas City, 1978.

———. *The Message of Evangelism: The Saving Power of God.* Kansas City: Beacon Hill Press, 1963.

Rodeheaver, Homer. *Twenty Years with Billy Sunday.* Winona Lake, Ind.: Rodeheaver Hall-Mack Co., 1936.

Rudolph, L. C. *Francis Asbury.* Nashville: Abingdon Press, 1966.

Ruffin, Bernard. *Fanny Crosby.* Philadelphia: United Church Press, 1976.

Sandall, Robert. *History of the Salvation Army.* London: Nelson Press, 1947.

Shirgwin, A. M. *The Bible in World Evangelism.* New York: Friendship Press, 1954.

Smith, Page. *The Nation Comes of Age: History of the Ante-Bellum Years.* Vol. 4 of *A People's History of the United States.* New York: McGraw-Hill Book Co., 1981.

Smith, Timothy L. *Called unto Holiness.* Vol. 1, *The Story of the Nazarenes: The Formative Years.* Kansas City: Nazarene Publishing House, 1962.

———. *Revivalism and Social Reform.* New York: Abingdon Press, 1957.

Soderwall, Loran Harris. "The Rhetoric of the Methodist Camp Meeting Movement, 1800-1850." Ph.D. diss., University of Southern California, 1971.

Sweazey, George E. *Effective Evangelism: The Greatest Work in the World.* New York: Harper and Row, 1953.

Sweet, William Warren. *Religion on the American Frontier: A Collection of Source Materials.* Vol. 4, *The Methodist, 1783-1840.* Chicago: University of Chicago Press, 1931—.

———. *Revivalism in America: Its Origin, Growth, and Decline.* New York: Charles Scribner's Sons, 1945.

———. *The Story of Religions in America.* New York: Harper and Brothers, 1939.

Taylor, Mendell. *Exploring Evangelism: History, Methods, Theology.* Kansas City: Beacon Hill Press, 1964.

Taylor, Richard Shelley. "The Doctrine of Sin in the Theology of Charles Grandison Finney." Th.D. diss., Boston University, 1953.

Thompson, William Oscar, Jr. "The Public Invitation as a Method of Evangelism: Its Origin and Development." Ph.D. diss., Southwestern Baptist Theological Seminary, 1979.

Tyerman, Luke. *The Life and Times of the Rev. John Wesley, M.A., Founder of the Methodists.* 2nd ed. 3 vols. London: Hodder and Stoughton, 1872-75.

Walker, Williston. *History of the Christian Church.* New York: Charles Scribner's Sons, 1959.

Walzer, William Charles. "Charles Grandison Finney and the Presbyterian Revivals of Central and Western New York." Ph.D. diss., University of Chicago, 1944.

Weisberger, Bernard A. *They Gathered at the River.* Boston: Little, Brown and Co., 1958.

Wesley, Charles. *The Journal of Charles Wesley.* London: Culley, 1909.

Wesley, John. *The Journal of John Wesley.* Vols. 1—4 of *The Works of John Wesley.* Edited by Thomas Jackson. 14 vols. 3rd ed. Reprint. Kansas City: Beacon Hill Press of Kansas City, 1978.

Whiteley, G. *Wesley's England.* London: Epworth Press, 1943.

Whitesell, Farris Daniel. *Basic New Testament Evangelism.* Grand Rapids: Zondervan Publishing House, 1949.

Wiley, H. Orton. *Christian Theology.* Vol. 1 of 3 vols. Kansas City: Beacon Hill Press of Kansas City, 1940.